GOD'S CODED LANGUAGE

"CRACKING THE CODE TO THE REALM OF PROPHETIC INTERPRETATION"

Misha Wesley

Misha Wesley/The Dreamers Publishing House

233 Henry Ave Suite 11
Memphis, TN 38104

www.republishing.org

Unless otherwise indicated, scripture is taken from the King James Version.'

Scripture quotations marked (NLT) are taken from the Holy Bible, New Living Translation, copyright ©1996, 2004, 2015 by Tyndale House Foundation. Used by permission of Tyndale House Publishers, Carol Stream, Illinois 60188. All rights reserved.

God's Coded Language/ Misha Wesley

ISBN-13: 9798724537346

TABLE OF CONTENTS

CHAPTER 1

SEERS, DREAMERS, VISIONARIES AND PROPHETS

Over the years, I've studied the characteristics of seers, Dreamers, visionaries and prophets. During that time, even now, I've seen many things we each have in common. All prophets are not Dreamers, but every prophet can dream. Every seer is not a prophet, but every seer can prophesy by the spirit of God. Every visionary are not prophets, but every prophet is a visionary. The goal of the distinction holy spirit led me to elaborate on, is not to create another doctrine by any means, however it's to bring clarity to the roles and functionalities of these gifts and administrations.

THE PROPHET

"I am a voice shouting in the wilderness, 'Clear the way for the Lord's coming!'" — John 1:22-23 (NLT)

Every prophet has their John the Baptist season. The season In which he feels like a voice shouting and no one hears. During this particular season, All they can do is interceed and weep. The Lord wants prophets in that posture because he wants us to forsake ourselves, Forsake our own flesh, our own desires and cry out in intercession.

Even apostles cry out! Don't think that once you become an Apostle your time of crying out in intercession gets easier or goes away! No, it gets worse! Our burdens get heavier, because there's much more at stake! We can discern the weight of the entire body of Christ!

I believe That's why Paul wrote so many letters, Because he always addressed the church as a whole. Which leads me to this; our duty is crying out, on our knees, in intercession, not seeking platforms.

We need to be reminded of who sent us! Don't get so caught up in life that you stop preparing and equipping the bride!

Apostles and prophets, the body needs us. It still has ways a way to go until it becomes established. The bride still needs to be prepared to fullness until we become ONE with the ABBA!

Throughout the scriptures, the word displays the characteristics of Prophets, the behavior of Prophets, the lifestyles of prophets, all the way down to the foods they've ate. The scriptures are very clear concerning the calling of the prophet.

CHAPTER 2

THE CALLING OF THE PROPHET

"I knew you before I formed you in your mother's womb. Before you were born I set you apart and appointed you as my prophet to the nations."—Jeremiah 1:5 (NLT)

Can the Lord be speaking to every believer in this scripture? Of course he can. However, it relates specifically to the calling of the prophet. The prophet's ministry is designed by God to help protect the church from the devices, attacks and plans of hell. God speaks through his Prophets and through them he sends his plans, messages, and wisdom. Some leaders and people in the church don't believe in the prophet's ministry because of misrepresentation or abuse and I get that, however, we can tell by the fruit, which means the character, of a true Prophet.

1 John 4:1, explains that We should try the spirit by the spirit, and every true prophet must possess the fruit of the spirit which is love, joy, peace, forbearance, kindness, gentleness, and most importantly self-control (Galatians 5:22). The true call of a prophet first starts with God choosing from the womb, whom he appoints as his Prophets. Then, the lord leads the Prophet on a journey of self-cleansing and healing of the heart.

The condition of the heart is God's biggest concern, Which leads us to walk in righteousness or in wickedness. If our hearts are after Christ, then out of our mouths will then pour the words of Christ and our lives will reflect the ways of our father in heaven. We also know that his ways are righteous and true.

The Prophet's ministry brings with it the power to preserve. In Hosea 12:13 And by a prophet the LORD brought Israel out of Egypt, and by a prophet was he preserved. The prophet's ministry is to guard, preserve, protect, and keep, which there is a Shamar aspect of a prophet's ministry of guarding; people, cities, regions and territories. Prophets are strong builders and restorers. You simply cannot stick prophets in the corner and say pray, only because prophets do much more in the body of Christ and are called to teach, train and equip, the body of Christ Ephesians 4:11.

We know the blueprints and patterns from heaven for building. The office of the prophet is more than just prophesying or singing great anointed songs, having visions and dreams, prophets water and bring refreshing, prophets bring correction; prophets have a strong releasing anointing, they help release people into their destiny.

In 1 Samuel, you notice the prophet Samuel was used by God to anoint David; 1 Samuel 16:13 and when Samuel anointed Saul; 1 Samuel 10:1. Prophets have a strong breakthrough anointing and a strong deliverance anointing. As Jeremiah 1:10, prophets are designed to root out spirits of wickedness and pull down strongholds built by the enemy, destroy walls and barriers, throw down, build and plant. Prophets break down hard walls and help others enter into new realms of the spirit. When Prophets prophesy, they speak God's word like fire and as a hammer! This hammer breaks the rock into pieces Jeremiah 23:29. The fire spoken of in Jeremiah 23:29 is a purifying type of fire, this fire is figurative for a corrective word that brings deliverance, which is healing.

The governmental authority, meaning they declare the promises of God into the person's life setting people into God's order where the foundation can be laid in the person's life as they speak. The person hears the word you're delivering because it's said with more authority that God has spiritually been imparted from heaven. This is what makes this ministry and office of the prophet more of a setting, and releasing, it is of God's governmental authority.

Prophets tend to have more visions, dreams, and are able to see into the spirit realm. When a prophet stands in the fullness of their office, they operate in words of wisdom, words of knowledge, and strong discerning of spirits. Many prophets are different but should bare the same fruit of the spirit and should ALL recognize Jesus Christ as Lord and savior!

WHAT PROPHETS ARE NOT!

I want to just break the confusion right now and distinguish between Prophets and Psychics. Psychics are demonic and operate through familiar spirits, and receive much of their information from demons. In the book of Acts 16:16 it speaks of Paul and Silas interacting with a slave girl in which could predict the future and foretell future events. This girl operated through a familiar spirit or divination, it angered Paul and he then proceeded to cast the demon out of the girl. Another Prophet, who actually wasn't considered a prophet at all, was balaam beginning in the 22nd chapter of Numbers. Balaam was considered a diviner, meaning he operated by much divination and sorcery. He actually made much of his wealth seeking ungodly assistance for many people including the king Balak.

The bible actually speaks of God turning his face against those who operate in witchcraft. Psychic's are a perverted form of a prophet. Because ALL true prophets get all their information from God. Any person that gets their Information from any other source, is not considered God's prophet but a false one.

CHAPTER 3

POEM FOR PROPHETS

The heart of the prophet is deep and with much tender care

We dream dreams and have visions

We fight tradition and religion

We pluck up and throw down

We overthrow church systems and programs

We build and plant

Prophets love the glory and the presence of god

We cry out to god with a glory chant

The prophet sees what no one else can't

the prophet stands out with ease

We're the insider that thinks like an outsider

Prophets are grieved by staleness and complacency

Prophets hate double mindedness and confusion

And A lukewarm church clouded with delusion

Prophets are not impressed with big buildings and fancy pews

Prophets love genuine repentance and when people are true

Prophets never compromise their beliefs to agree with the world

We walk in the spirit and rebuke lusts of the flesh

Prophets are intercessors and prayer warriors

We push and inspire

We encourage others to bring out their fire

Prophets are fanatical over the top and radical

Prophets are not naysayers and people pleasers!

God always takes care of his prophets

Providing love and much protection

Our cups overflow with favor and progression

Were conquerors and warriors

Were victors and never victims

Arise prophets and come out of your caves you're hiding ends here!

The deliverance for america is near !

CHAPTER 4

THE SEER

Seers are an extremely critical part of the body of Christ. Being the eyes of Christ, seers are equipped to see beyond the natural realm, and I mean beyond seeing just you and me; a.ka "human interaction". Christ opens their eyes to see pain in certain places of the body that needs to be healed. Seers will see in the spirit potential attacks, hindrances and opposition from the enemy. For example;

While on assignment at work, a coworker, asked me to pray for her. However, as she approached me, I could see a heaviness on her shoulders, as if there were literal hands on her shoulders, bearing down on them. So, as I began to pray, it turned into a healing session of removing false burdens from off her shoulders, the spirit of heaviness, the spirit of oppression and depression. The more I prayed, she began to cry and weep and nod her head in agreement the entire time.

When I was done, she asked me, "are you some kind of prophet?" I calmly said yes and released into her the love of the father as i hugged her.

In the passage above, I gave an example, of How you can know for certain that you are a Seer. however, What are the differences between a Seer and a prophet? Are they the same?

The only way for you to know the difference is to simplify the two administrations and to pull from both the new, and the old testament definitions.

1 Samuel 9:9 KJV

(Beforetime in Israel, when a man went to enquire of God, thus he spake, Come, and let us go to the seer: for he that is now called a Prophet was before time called a Seer.)

If we look at this verse, Every prophet is not a dreamer of dreams and every Seer is not a prophet. Look closely at 1 Corinthians 12:4 There are different kinds of spiritual gifts, but the same Spirit is the source of them all. There are different kinds of service, but we serve the same Lord. God works in different ways, but it is the same God who does the work in all of us. —1 Corinthians 12:4-6 NLT

It is extremely important to note that seers are not a governmental office, however, the prophet is. The prophet is appointed to build the foundations, which takes a specific governmental authority to establish decrees in the earth realm. There may be seers who have been saved longer, meaning they've been walking with christ longer, baptized for more years than the prophet, however, it is the governmental authority that has more weight in the realm of the spirit. You can't simply decide to be a prophet or force the office, because the authority or weight of the anointing is measured by God himself. Seers operate at a much different capacity giving them the ability to see sometimes what the prophet can't.

God has given seers a different dimensional scope of the prophetic realm, which in return, makes them have an immense amount of visions, Both open-eyed and closed-eyed. Seers can see pictures in their mind's eye, meaning God can show them a picture or even have a vision while they're looking at someone, and God does this because he has a message for that person.

The eyes of the seer are used by Christ to communicate his message to the church (side note, when

I say church, that's not only limited to those who are in a church building or setting). a seer can be at work, at the bookstore, or at the grocery store, and still receive important messages for a person that god wants to speak to. Although I am a seer, my predominant operation is hearing. Meaning God deals with me more audibly. When God wants me to prophesy to someone, he will audibly whisper it into my ear or into my mind. However, depending on the person, I would operate in either a vision, a picture, or the voice of the lord.

The Seer can identify an area of the body a person needs to be physically healed, The seer can identify when strongholds need to be broken and deliverance needs to take place. Which brings me to the very special gift of discerning of spirits only given to a select few of believers. In its simplest form, this gifting is specifically in full operation during deliverance because it is a gifting for that purpose. The seer is extremely detrimental to the ministry of deliverance because they see what other can't. Their may be a demonic spirit holding onto a person and not wanting to let go and the seer may have the ability to catch that. During deliverance, Seers can see demonic spirits being expelled from the person, seers can identify specific Angel's of the lord as they come. As you imagine, how in the world can we operate without seers?

WORD ORIGINS

Perhaps we should begin by looking at some of the Hebrew words translated in Scripture as "prophet" and "seer." The Strong's Concordance translates these as follows:

"SEER" Hebrew (7200, 7203, 2374, 2372)

- Hebrew 7200: ra'ah, raw-aw'; to see, look, view; to realize, know, consider; to be selected; to become visible, appear, show oneself; to be seen; to cause to see, show; to be shown; to look at each other, meet with; a general word for visual perception.
- Hebrew 7203: ro'eh, ro-eh'; a seer; vision.
- Hebrew 2374: Chozeh, kho-zeh'; seer, one who receives a communication from God, with a possible focus that the message had a visual component; agreement.

- Hebrew 2372: Chazah, khaw-zaw'; to see, to look, observe, gaze, by extension: to choose (one thing or another); to have visions, to prophesy.

"PROPHET" Hebrew (5030, 5012, 5197)

- Hebrew 5030: nabiy', naw-bee'; a prophet (true or false).

- Hebrew 5012: naba', naw-baw'; to prophesy, speak as a prophet; prophecy has its focus on encouraging or restoring covenant faithfulness, the telling of future events encourages obedience or warns against disobedience.

- Hebrew 5197: nataph, naw-taf'; to pour down; gently fall, drip; to (drip words) preach, prophesy.

WORD USAGE

We also need to look at how the words are used. Many use the terms "seer" and "prophet" interchangeably. Furthermore, some believe that seers have not existed since the time of the Prophet Samuel (1150 B.C. – 1010 B.C.). They quote 1 Samuel 9:9: "(Formerly in Israel, when a man went to inquire of God, he spoke thus: 'Come, let us go to the seer' for he who is now called a prophet was formerly called a seer)".

However, this is a shortsighted point of view and creates a dilemma: Why does Scripture continue to make a distinction between prophets and seers after the era of Samuel?

SEERS AND PROPHETS CONTINUE TO CO-EXIST

I believe that seers and prophets continue to "co-exist" throughout Scripture. Both Gad, the seer, and Nathan, the prophet, served in King David's court (2 Samuel 24:4; 1 Chronicles 29:29). Asaph, the seer, and Isaiah, the prophet, were also contemporaries during King Hezekiah's reign (2 Chronicles 29:30; 2 Kings 20:1).

Therefore, I believe that 1 Samuel 9:9 implies that Samuel moved from functioning as a seer to functioning as a prophet. Or, more likely that Samuel fulfilled both the functions of a seer and a prophet!

In addition, there seems to be a difference even between those who functioned as "seers". In 1 Chronicles 29:29, the word "seer" is used twice, but it is not the same Hebrew word. "Now the acts of King David, first and last, indeed they are written in the book of Samuel the seer (7200), in the book of Nathan the prophet (5030), and in the book of Gad the seer (2374)" (1 Chronicles 29:29). Perhaps this indicates a difference in how Samuel and Gad received revelation from God.

SAMUEL'S VS. GAD'S EXPERIENCES

Samuel had a wide variety of revelatory experiences, perhaps broader than Gad's. Samuel was gifted in visions, knowings, and dreams. He transcended time and geographic locality to watch events that were occurring simultaneously outside of his immediate geographic location. He knew who was coming to his door before the person arrived. He even predicted weather patterns (1 Samuel 12:17).

In contrast, Gad's revelatory gift was not as well documented. It is possible that he walked in the same level of prophetic gifting as Samuel, but there is no record of this. Scripture indicates that he carried the Lord's rebuke to David for numbering Israel (2 Samuel 24:11-13). He also helped arrange Levitical music (2 Chronicles 9:25), and apparently wrote a history book about David's reign (1 Chronicles 29:29).

Did people go to a seer more than to a prophet? It seemed to be common practice for the people of Israel to look to the seers for direction (1 Samuel 9:6-9). It was also common for them to bring the seer an offering for his livelihood (1 Samuel 9:7). There are also several instances where people went to the prophet for wisdom and direction from God.

In conclusion, prophets and seers still function today, as they did in biblical times. In fact we are seeing a worldwide renaissance in these types of revelatory gifts. Next month, I will offer deeper insights on these dynamic, re-emerging, and mysterious revelatory gifts.

The sons of issachar taken from 1 chronicles 12:32 and (a revivalists heart):

The Sons of Issachar were those that knew which season it was. This sounds like a family gifting passed passed on from Issachar, a son of Jacob, to the next generation and by possible implication to further generations. It was a spiritual ability that was modelled by Issachar and taught to his offspring. Others were aware of it and came to inquire as to the 'season', that is they came to ask for guidance as to which course of action would prosper and which would not. This is a seer/prophetic type of anointing which contained a good measure of Spiritual discernment and revelation.

Why is it still important for the Issachar anointing to be relevant today?

Let's look at the key words in 1 Chronicles 12:32

"And of the children of Issachar, which were men that had understanding of the time, to know what Israel ought to do; the heads of them were two hundred; and all their brethren were at their commandment."

Issachar – The meaning of this name is "he will bring reward, man for hire"

Men– a person, people

Understanding – to separate mentally, to distinguish, be cunning, diligently, deal wisely, be prudent

Times – fortunes, occurrences. Fortunes mean success, prosperity, estates, possessions, wealth. Occurrence means an event, an incident, happenings, circumstance.

Know – to know or ascertain by seeing. The Hebrew word know in this verse is yada, which is word that means god gives personal understanding and revelation, and is not a knowing that comes from reading a book for example.

By virtue of the name, we see that those who walk in the character and calling of the Issachar anointing bring a sure reward to the Lord as well as a reward to the vineyard in which they are working. Their mind is cunning, able to mentally distinguish between that which is wise and unwise. They diligently pursue understanding needed to live well before the Lord. Issachar men and women receive understanding from the Lord himself, because they know God in an intimate manner. Because they are wise and prudent. Issachar's are able to perceive and seize opportune times of success and wealth.

This is the anointing needed to sustain revival. The anointing that births Kingdom financiers who are able to find wealth and offer it back as a sacrifice to God. This generation need to become wiser and more strategic in their thinking. It is not enough for us to just be pew warmers or just considered with getting positions in church. God is calling for an increase of His government throughout the world. His is busy training those who are willing to be stewards of wealth and to not become selfish in the process. The prophets will become younger with age and so those birthing the next generation we cannot let this anointing rest. It must walked to accompany the signs and wonders. It is just as much supernatural as miracles and signs to be able to discern what God is doing and to be able to run with Him in that season.

So what season is it now?
A season of growing Global visitation by God
A season of empowerment of the saints

A season to open ancient wells and to old and new cluster anointing – Oil has been discovered in Israel. Israel will now become fully sustainable. That well was opened.

A season to re-envision and to dream big dream again

A season to release another generation into the end time purposes

A season to make bold requests at the Throne Room

A season for those who believe in God to do exploits

This is a very exciting time to be born in. Let's not waste it on idle talk but see what God is doing around the world and how we can be apart of it. Let's get into Gods chamber and ask Him. We want more of this anointing passed on to us and future generations. Issachar were the chief advisors to the Kings. Let us touch the people of influence with the knowledge and revelation of God.

VISIONARIES

A VISIONARY is an inspired leader. they are consistently driven by their ambitious plans for the future. a visionary sees the possible future or potential beauty of what could be for a business, a company or church, and then builds according to the blueprints given. The genetic makeup of a visionary comes straight from the father. The lord provides blueprints that only a visionary can read and interpret. The dreamer may dream or have the ability to see what the lord is doing, however, it takes the visionary to build the vision. this dna is demonstrated in the lives of those who call themselves kingdom-preneurs, entrepreneurs, solopreneurs, and soulpreneurs. Visionary people can visualize things easily. When you talk to visionary leaders, you can recognize them from the rest of the crowd because of their imagination. Visionaries can imagine future possibilities in their minds and then explain what they have imagined clearly. They imagine things that others cannot imagine. Through their imagination, they can draw future possibilities for their organization. You can recognize visionaries by their ability to see the big picture. In a group of people, visionary ones talk about the big picture and how various factors link together to create that picture. They see the whole process and not a single step.

Since visionary leaders are big-picture oriented, they are not attached. They are not worried about why this happened and why that did not happen. They enjoy the whole process. They are patient. They see all the links in the big picture and therefore they do not blame others.When you are in presence of a true visionary, you can feel their power. Visionaries are powerful because they are focused and present. In other words, focus and presence create power.

Since visionaries are present and focused, you can connect with them when they talk about what they have in mind, when they teach you something, or when they perform a task. People are more drawn to those who are focused and present. That is why visionaries have more followers. As mentioned earlier, true visionaries see what others cannot see. They see the big picture. They see the links among different events. They see possible obstacles. They know there would be challenges along the way. They know they might have temporary setbacks. But they also know the great value of fulfilling the vision. Therefore, true visionaries never give up. They are not afraid of failures because they know that failures are part of the process as well.

In a group of leaders, true visionaries can be recognized with their tendency towards taking risks and transforming those risks to opportunities. Their positive approach and their focus on the vision help them not be afraid of failures. Such leaders are willing to discover new paths and become searchlights for others. This is the secret of their success.

I believe the DNA of a visionary is installed only in remnants who desire to build what isn't easy, what others think is impossible. the visionary builds from within. we understand that nothing the lord does begins outward but begins inward. If we look at the building patterns of moses, we know that the lord built moses in the wilderness spiritually, and delivered him so that he may be effective in then delivering an entire nation from the grip of pharaoh. If we look in the book of joshua, joshua is seen as a visionary. as he leads the entire nation of israel into the promised land, the entire time he is seen getting direct instructions from the lord. the blueprints was given to him by god. at every major turn, he is consulting with god for battle strategies, identifying achan, who kept the items that was set apart for the lord after the battle of jericho, which is begins in Joshua 7,

One of the big signs of visionaries is their willingness for sharing their vision with the world. They don't keep it to themselves because they know that they cannot get to the destination alone. They need others for filling the gaps and that is why they communicate their vision and dreams with others to attract the right people.

Visionaries can also be named pattern makers. Apostles and some prophets can flow heavily in this area. They are the ones to receive the plans, architecturally of how god wants a certain business, or church to function. Jesus is the ultimate pattern maker because he's already set the pattern in motion for how the new testament church should function. he did this by exemplifying this standard in the book of acts, the look, the feel, and the very plans of how each church should operate.

THE RIVER OF THE PROPHETIC

"He that believeth on me, as the scripture hath said, out of his belly shall flow rivers of living water". John 7:38

"The prophetic is a river and the river is the life of the prophetic, the word of God breeds knowledge and understanding into the Prophetic"

I fell in love with the word of God and in love with every word the scriptures held. The word of God became my bread day and night. I studied to shew thyself approved (2 Timothy 2:15) and when I say this I truly mean it.

I would read the scriptures and desire to walk them out, teach them, preach them, lead through them. I studied them so much I compared versions, studied and The Heart Of A Young Prophet researched concepts and biblical history. I literally became obsessed with God and wanted to be with him all the time in prayer. God wants us to fall in love with him and be submerged into his presence. I fell in love with God over and over and over again. The love and intimacy I feel for Christ and him dying for my sins is the ultimate sacrifice! My heart swells for the prophetic and I coveted to prophesy. to covet something, means you yearn to possess it or to have it.

I sought to prophesy and did not desire or covet the things of this world. To covet something means to yearn to possess or to have it really bad; but we can covet to prophesy and desire spiritual gifts all day long according to 1 Corinthians 14:39. however, ultimately it's your hunger that will drive your to be better, go deeper, and stay in a low place, being completely humbled before the father and the world.

I desired to be better than my former self. I was speaking to a young lady about being aligned with an Apostle as opposed with a pastor, or preacher. Not that anything is wrong with pastors and preachers I love them. We all love them. However, being aligned with the right apostolic leader helps us to better understand our calling in ministry, our direction in ministry, they help teach us, release us and equip us for the calling that God placed on our lives. It's imperative as a prophet of the most High God, that I am aligned spiritually with a strong apostolic covering that can watch my growth and development spiritually, challenge me and groom me to be better. I feel as a prophet we cannot be lone rangers, wandering without a covering. Rebellion can plague anybody, especially prophets, and Spiritual protection for God's people depends completely upon proper positioning. The Power of Prayer is one key area that allows us covering as I explained in previous chapters. It's through my prayers, decrees and covering my family with the Blood of Jesus Christ, that all the people around me were protected and safe from harm of the evil one. Another example is Divinely appointed relationships. Divine relationships are those relationships God uses and appoints, to allow proper grooming, maturing and better spiritual health. "Then the Lord will provide shade for Mount Zion and all who assemble there. He will provide a canopy of cloud during the day and smoke and flaming fire at night, covering the glorious land. It will be a shelter from daytime heat and a hiding place from storms and rain" Isaiah 4:5-6. In verse 5, "Then the Lord will provide shade for Mount Zion and all who assemble there", this is the actual churches, the assemblies of God. I praise the Lord that he is raising up Apostolic and prophetic leaders in this season that are truly after heart of God.

We must make it our mission to get into an environment and around a company of Prophets and prophetic leaders that stirs up our gifts, our worship, our prayer lives, challenges us to be better and to lead more holy and righteous lives. We must be around other prophetic people and prophets because it's to my knowledge and according to scripture when we get around other prophetic people, it is definitely contagious! 1 Corinthians 14:1, in the KJV, it says, "Follow after charity and desire spiritual gifts, but rather that ye may prophesy." The King James version states that we should desire spiritual gifts, but the true gift is the Holy Spirit and you should know that in the original translation gifts was not in there.

Instead the NLT says, "Let love be your highest goal! But you should also desire the special abilities the Spirit gives--especially the ability to prophesy." This scripture allows us to know that the Holy spirit is the one who gives us special abilities and we should desire to prophesy. A desire is a desperate need to have, to lust after with the heart. God wants us to desire and lust to prophecy and for the spiritual gifts. There are diversities of gifts, but the same spirit and there are differences of administrations but the same Lord (1 Corinthians 14:4,5). The gifts of the spirit are wisdom, knowledge, faith, healing, the workings of miracles, the gift of prophecy, discerning of spirits, divers kinds of tongues and the gift of interpretation of tongues. The prophetic is a river and the river is the life of the prophetic, the word of God breeds knowledge and understanding into the Prophetic. Prophecy is a river that flows from your belly. A figurative river that can only be seen and observed with spiritual eyes.

The atmosphere in prophetic churches needs to be unlike anything anyone has ever experienced. this atmosphere needs to be charged with the love of abba and filled with worship. our churches need to be filled with the glory of the lord, so that when non believers can come encounter and be Free to be who abba designed them to be. they can be free to sing and free to dance. i'm not just saying that they should sing a really good song from an old hymn book and sit down, not that there's anything wrong with doing that, however, we really need to be pressed into the spirit of God, the river of heaven, waiting for the spirit of the lord to come strongly. "Because where the spirit of the lord is there is freedom"— 2 Corinthians 3:17.

As we press in and worship singing the songs of the Lord, we allowed the word of God to Nataph which is a Hebrew word meaning to drop, let drop, to prophesy! then your leaders, who are prophetic, usually, minstrels, apostles, or prophets can rise up and prophesy, then others can stand up and prophesy as well. this establishes, the order and fulfills the scripture,"Let the prophets speak two or three, and let the other Judge."– 1 Corinthians 14:29

When the presence of God is welcomed into worship, it allows his word to build up then drop onto us while in service. As the word drops it falls like rain onto his prophetic people and we prophesy by the unction of the spirit one by one.

This atmosphere will be extremely conducive to the growth of new prophets and developing prophetic people who want to prophesy. this consistent atmosphere, will create a strong prophetic flow just like a river. When the Lord puts his word in the mouths of some prophets, they begin to operate more Nabiy than anything. This is a Hebrew Word meaning "to bubble forth, like a fountain"; the word flow out of you, until its complete, similar to faucet that's on full force then turned off letting drips come out then finally, the drips come to a stop these types of prophets announce or pour forth the declarations of God. The word in them becomes like a pot of boiling water, building up to its hottest point and bubbling forth. When they feel the unction to prophesy to someone God tells them to speak to, the word becomes so strong and they'll feel compelled by his hand to deliver that word.

I remember years ago, i was at the gas station waiting in line to pay for gas. In front of me stood this tall heavy muscle-built man. For some reason I could only look at his legs which were large and massive. Then I heard the Lord say "I shall trample upon the lion and adder: the young lion and dragon thou shalt trample under foot", Psalms 91:13. Then I saw him in the spirit literally stepping on these creatures with these his massive legs. In the spirit I saw him carrying armor upon his back. As I went back to my car, I felt the strong unction and the word bubbling up in my belly to prophesy to him. I stood by my car and contemplated not to, then the Lord said if you don't, you'll be disobedient to my instruction.

Not wanting to be disobedient to my father, I called to the man and immediately delivered the word. Turned out he was an MMA fighter for a living and literally fought in real life. He told me he was Hebrew and that the word was a blessing and on time. It doesn't matter whether we be Jews or Gentiles, whether we be bond or free, we have been all made to drink into one spirit, 1 Corinthians 12:13. The prophetic is the God encounter America needs; it's the encounter we've all been waiting for. Because the prophetic is not just some person's belief about your life but it is truly from the Holy Spirit. In the last days, God says, 'I will pour out my Spirit upon all people. Your sons and daughters will prophesy. Your young men will see visions, and your old men will dream dreams", Acts 2:17. God wants ALL PEOPLE TO PROPHESY, and God has ALREADY POURED OUT HIS SPIRIT!

If you have ever been apart of a prophetic activation, you can truly sense the strong presence of the Holy spirit and the atmosphere as there are almost thousands of people prophesying over one another. When I say that the prophetic is a God encounter, I mean we can hear the words that God is saying to us specifically. As they listen, their secret thoughts will be exposed, and they will fall to their knees and worship God, declaring, "God is truly here among you" 1 Corinthians 14:25.

All the scriptures are prophetic and the prophetic is what speaks to the heart, the will, and the intentions of God. You become his mouthpiece. Then the LORD reached out his hand and touched my mouth and said to me, «I have put my words in your mouth", Jeremiah 1:9. when you enter into the prophetic realm, your river begins to flow stronger and stronger with every utterance. But it takes faith to strengthen that flow. For without faith it is impossible to please God, Hebrews 11:1. To move in the gifts of the spirit takes courage, boldness and faith and without these, our gifts will lay stagnant, and dormant. Living in the spirit is what purifies us, and walking in righteousness and holiness brings us closer to god and worthy enough to be his mouthpiece. We are all spirit beings and to have a pure prophetic utterance. We cannot live in the flesh because the flesh was crucified on the cross when Jesus died, Mark 15:25. He died in the flesh and rose from the dead on the 3rd day in spirit, and it's his spirit which resides in us!

PRAYING IN TONGUES.

I want to elaborate on the subject of speaking in tongues. There was a time in my life, years ago, which I was unable to speak in other languages or in diversities of tongues as the Apostle Paul states in the book of Corinthians. However, I desired God so much, my hunger for him grew to astronomical levels, so All I wanted was his word and everything he wanted to offer me. My husband's cousin was very encouraging, and told me I needed to ask earnestly for the gift and our father would give. At that time in my life, I was extremely surprised that God would give such a beautiful utterance to me so quickly without me doing anything in return. He is a God that gives freely!

Praying in tongues are mysteries to men but a clear line of communication to The Father, 1 Corinthians

14:2. When we speak to him in our heavenly language, The Holy Spirit takes control of our tongue and then begins praying the PERFECT PRAYER. The enemy cannot understand what we say, some people cannot understand either, unless they interpret what the tongues say. Now if you have not received this wonderful gift from the Holy Spirit, do not fret thyself any longer, but instead ask the Father who gives to each one of us diligently as we ask. Speaking in tongues is a clear line of communication to the father. There is a gift of interpretation of tongues that God has graced to many and God has graced me to carry this gift of interpretation. In Acts 2:4 everyone present in the room became filled with the Holy Spirit and began speaking in tongues (New Living Translation calls it, "other Languages") So on the day of Pentecost, which came 50 days after the Passover, when Jesus was crucified) all of the Apostles were filled with the Spirit of Christ, which is his Holy Spirit or Holy Ghost (same thing), and all spoke in tongues. If you have been baptized (Born again) YOU CAN SPEAK IN TONGUES!

Psychologically, when we speak in tongues there is a part of our brain that relaxes and literally calms. A Neuroscientific study from the University of Pennsylvania as well as Reports from the New York Times, has been done on five women, as they spoke in tongues and sang prophetic songs. According to their research, as they spoke in tongues and found that their frontal lobes the thinking, willful part of the brain through which people control what they do were relatively quiet, as were the language centers.

The regions involved in maintaining self-consciousness were active. The women were not in blind trances, and it was unclear which region was driving the behavior. I love when science backs up what God does within us that cancels out the voices of all the naysayers and critical spirits in the world! These are quite astounding evidence that reveals God's abilities and strength, therefore, I assure you it is not spooky or weird, but powerful!

THE PROPHETIC REALM OF DREAMS, AND VISIONS

Visions reveal God's nature and they reveal God's blueprints and how he wants something constructed in the earth and the architectural pattern of how God desires something to be built.

Dreams are something we all have, as individuals, adults, children as well as the entire Human race. However, the context and symbolism of the dream can sometimes leave the dreamer puzzled or even a bit confused. As some try to reduce the dream into interpret its complexity with their natural mind. The problem some have with interpreting their own dream is that they digest the dream as a whole and interpret its meaning based off of emotions, feelings, actual life experiences, comparing and contrasting literal or natural symbols.

We also must be careful releasing dreams without first asking ABBA father for the interpretation of the dream. Some dreams come from the enemy, and once you open your mouth to release the dream, you could be releasing toxicity into your atmosphere and decreeing the very words of Satan.

The spirit of Wisdom and the spirit of knowledge from God, is definitely needed as we interpret our dreams. The number one mission of "School of Prophetic Arts and Worship", my equipping ministry and college I established, is That all watchman's Be on guard, having the spirit of wisdom and knowledge from the father, to decree and declare his word, on time and in season!

Although dreaming is common, every dream contains an uncommon prophetic message for each particular dreamer in which God engraves the message on their hearts. Its hidden message contains a problem encoded with a spiritual solution for each and every circumstance that will; guide, direct, keep, warn, foresee, foretell, hold, unlock and counsel.

Dream in Hebrew is Chalam-pronounced khaw-lam and means to be made strong; healthy. The Greek Lexicon meaning of dream is Onar; ovap- meaning an uncertain derivation; to dream, in a dream. So now we see here a deeper compelling comparison between these words as it is translated from English to Hebrew and Greek. Now let's take a look at the word "derivation" which means; obtaining or developing of something from a source or origin.

Therefore, it is a true statement that dreams can make us healthy and strong only if we know the derivation of its original source of the actual dream. Which brings me to dream sources and its origination.

Different dreams can be sorted into 3 different categories which then can be broken down into sub-categories in which determine the actual summary of the dream. For example:

1. Prophetic Dreams
2. Flesh Dreams
3. Dreams from the enemy

And then these dreams are placed into sub-categories, for example;
1. Prophetic Dreams: Calling dreams; warning dreams.

*Calling dreams: These dreams are usually filled with color, highly symbolic and the setting can be in unusual places.

Example of a prophetic dream/calling dream

Dream: I was inside a lobby, and i knew it was an architectural office. The office had architecture templates as displays in a table, and i was standing close to a door.

I knew in my dream i was inside an office, inside another big building. i saw business people around, I was dressed professional but i don't recall the clothing.

Suddenly this young very beautiful guy enter the office dressed in a cream suit color and he had curly hair, and he was very sharp.(that was my impression in the dream) I then saw myself walking with him, and during my walk, i saw the floor was white marble, and in-front a big glass window and lots of lighting. i also saw stairs going down, but my focus was in the big glass in-front of me, as i was holding a kid. Suddenly there was a big shake! and I saw him holding a small template with the same designed of a glass roof, that broke. He said, I'm looking for the architect that will build a strong house for you, so when the shake comes you are save. I don't recall anymore.

I was thinking is this dream referring to my faith or maybe a big shake its coming and the Lord its trying to put me in a save place. I don't know and haven't really pray about it. I only think that guy was an angel, but again I do need help to get the interpretation.

Thank you sister in Christ.

Interpretation:Hey woman of God!

First of let me say this is definitely a calling dream. The lord is calling you to your purpose. The lord has called you to the mountain of business. Let's break this down so that you can clearly understand your calling/instructions from the lord.

I was inside a lobby, and i knew it was an architectural office. The office had architecture templates as displays in a table.

This architectural scenery and templates represents that you are in a season of building. a season in which the lord will give you the heavenly blueprints and instructions for how to build, design and where you should go.

I was standing close to a door.This door represented an access point in the spirit. the lord says it's your door!

Suddenly this young very beautiful guy enter the office dressed in a cream suit color and he had curly hair, and he was very sharp.(that was my impression in the dream) I then saw myself walking with him. This man was in fact an angel, and the awesome thing about angels is that he is assigned to give you the assignment. God has given his angel charge over you! Psalms 91:11. The angel has been assigned to help you design!! The lord is giving you the blueprints to design a business for the business mountain, (I knew in my dream i was inside an office, inside another big building. i saw business people around).

This part of your dream symbolized a just this! For the marketplace, God has given you a unique and creative idea. and this shaking is a SPIRITUAL AWAKENING!! The shaking will shake you to your very spiritual core! It's not a bad shaking but a good shaking! praise God!

I then saw myself walking with him, and during my walk, walking or running in your dream symbolizes your faith (we walk by faith not by sight 2 Corinthians 5:7) and also your spiritual endurance, because of the scripture that says, "The shall walk and not faint."— Isaiah 40:31

I saw the floor was white marble, and in-front a big glass window and lots of lighting this symbolizes a heavenly place/ heavenly realm, hence the lighting, the marble floors. The glass windows represents the open revelations or visions God will show you concerning this creative business idea!

I also saw stairs going down, but my focus was in the big glass in-front of me, as i was holding a kid. I love this part of the dream; because you wasn't focused on the stairs which were going down meaning "negativity" or "downfall" or "demotion" your focus was on the revelation, the vision, the big picture that God was showing you!! Also, the child you were holding represents this creative idea the lord has given, the gifts he's called for you to care for and protect, amen!

I'm holding a small template with the same designed of a glass roof, that broke. He said, I'm looking for the architect that will build a strong house for you.This part of the dream represents an area in which you were hurt or weakened. Your spiritual ceiling was shattered as a result and the lord is rebuilding you stronger than you were before so that you may be able to withstand future attack.

All of the dreams i have had the honor of interpreting, by the power of the Holy Spirit, has provided direction, correction, what is happening now and a prophetic word of what will come in the future.

*Warning dreams will show you of an event that is taking place or about to take place. This would be God exposing something that is often hidden, dangerous, or potentially dangerous to you or those around you. God gives us these types of dreams because we sometimes cannot see what satan is planning with our natural eyes. These dreams assist us in revealing the hidden snares of satan.

EXAMPLE OF A WARNING DREAM

I saw my self driving in many many many Lane's like highways and in the back there was a baby girl crying..and in the passenger side some dude that's in my church teaching and telling me where to go then I don't know if you're familiar with a kid show called Reading Rainbow but all of the sudden the church dude was sitting in a small stool chair and had this big book it was open on his lap and coming out of the pages was beams of bright rainbow colors and he seem to be telling or trying to teach me something this dream was not control by me and it happened so fast and felt so peaceful I woke up and got ready for work but it was the last dream I dream that day before work and it was so vivid ...I want to know if it was a lustful and fleshy dream, or from God or from the enemy and what does it mean?

Interpretation: So here's the interpretation;
Right off the bat, I'll tell you that this dream was from God and God was actually "Warning you".

I saw my self driving in many many many Lane's like highways and in the back there was a baby girl crying

This part of the dream symbolizes the gift god has given to you, the baby was crying, meaning you've forgotten about it and you've allowed those God sized dreams to take a back seat. As I was reading over this dream I heard the word "entrepreneur", "vision" like God has given you this massive dream or business idea to steward and you've actually been "misguided" regarding that.

There's some voices in the church that you've allowed to speak into your life in reference to that and it has you "in the wrong Lane" God is saying to stay in your lane...let me not get ahead of myself but please keep reading.

..and in the passenger side some dude that's in my church teaching and telling me where to go then I don't know if you're familiar with a kid show called Reading Rainbow but all of the sudden the church dude was sitting in a small stool chair and had this big book it was open on his lap and coming out of the pages was beams of bright rainbow colors and he seem to be telling or trying to teach me something this dream was not control by me

This is the part of the dream in which I meant, you've allowed some voices in the church to speak into your life that have a "small position" in the spirit (hence the small chair/stool=small/tiny position) the fact that you were driving the car meant that you WERE IN CONTROL the WHOLE TIME however, you allowed this guy to point you in the direction he wanted you to go and that's why God said to STAY IN THE LANE I'VE PLACED YOU IN! Don't be at peace with anyone dictating the direction your life is going besides the holy spirit.

Get alone with God and seek him. Seek him for this vision, or entrepreneurial sized goal.

I'm praying for you dreamer!

3. Dreams from the Enemy: Fear Dreams; dreams that are dark in nature

*The dreams from the enemy would be the dreams that do not line up with God's word. If the enemy seeks to steal, kill and destroy, John 10:10, then the dream realm would be no exception. Since we cannot be ignorant to satan's devices, we must learn to arm

ourselves. meaning to cover ourselves with prayer and the blood of Jesus which protects us even when the enemy tries to hit us with his best shot!

4.   Flesh dreams/Soulish, self-Conditioning: The majority of these dreams come straight from our own mind, and our own repressed or suppressed emotions. These dreams that denote the condition of our heart and dreamer itself. Did you know that eating certain food before sleeping or taking certain medications can affect your dream life and how well you transition through sleep cycles?

The dream realm helps to aid us to go deeper into the realms of the spirit. If you're a dreamer, than you should be overjoyed because you have an advantage over the enemy, he thinks your not paying attention to. The dream realm helps us to go deep into the heart of God, into the deep realms of the spirit and search for the Lord's wisdom, power and might.

Just like every dreamer won't be the same, every dream and vision won't be the same. A dreamer can dream of what I call a 3-fold dream, in which contains different types of dreams rolled into one. Meaning one part can be prophetic, the other part can be a flesh and another part can be a self-conditioning. Depending on the dreamers' spiritual state will determine the dreams length, category and sub-category. You see dreams are not a one size fits all!

Dreams are never just "silly dreams", no matter how insignificant others or even you may think that dream is, it will always reveal your thought life, health, love life, heart, flesh, spiritual walk, people around you and their hidden motives. The deeper connected you are to the heart of God, the more secrets God will whisper and reveal to you in your dreams!

Not only will God reveal to us his secrets in dreams, but he will reveal them in visions and especially in numbers. Numbers are like a code, a combination lock to a safe and behind the combination lock, behind the door is hidden treasure waiting to be found! I believe it was extremely necessary for me to write a section on every topic of; dreams, visions and numbers.

I have seen people try to interpret numbers, however, it bothered me because they were just scratching the surface of a topic in which God wanted us to dig deeper on, then expand upon it. Every single Number interpretation I have done for anyone has been confirmed to be truth by the person who first allowed me to interpret it.

I don't believe that God gives dreams, visions, or show us repetitive number sequences, for us to simply dream, however, it's to Ignite us, inspire us, warn us, direct us, and also, at times, free us!

Therefore, the gift of interpretation is not just a gift for me to hold onto and simply interpret dreams, However, it's to equip you to use your dreams, visions and numbers, to pray strategically over your regions, families, businesses, jobs, children, finances, and ministries. God actually combines visions, dreams and numbers to actually unlock prayer strategies, divine plans and prophetic symbols and blueprints. Think of it this way, our lives are like one big literal puzzle and the more the pieces come together, the more the pictures make sense. Once we discover the "Jesus piece" we ultimately uncover a missing part of ourselves. Then we are not to just stop there, but to continue on. That "Jesus Piece" is only a doorway into all that he has for you! Remember this:

It is the glory of God to conceal a thing: but the honor of kings is to search out a matter. –Proverbs 25:2

CHAPTER 7

THE REVELATORY REALM

THE WORD OF KNOWLEDGE:

This form of knowledge only comes from God. This knowledge is supernatural and know facts supernaturally. The gift of the Word of Knowledge refers to the ability to know facts about a situation or a spiritual principle that could not have been known by natural means. This allows someone to see a situation as God sees it. John 4:16-19 points to a perfect example of a Samaritan woman that comes to the well where Jesus was sitting to get water. Jesus said to her, "Go, call your husband, and come here." The woman answered him, "I have no husband." Jesus said to her, "You are right in saying, 'I have no husband'; for you have had five husbands, and the one you now have is not your husband. What you have said is true." The woman said to him, "Sir, I perceive that you are a prophet. John 4:16-19 (ESV)

This is an example of a Word of Knowledge. How else could have Jesus known this information without the woman telling him? It was by the Word of Knowledge that manifested by the spirit that was upon Jesus! A word of knowledge can manifest by the spirit through a vision (mental picture; either opened eye or closed eye), hearing God's voice, or through a dream that the spirit of God has quickened to your spirit. The Word of Knowledge and understanding will always work together. Meaning, God will not give you a Word of Wisdom without giving you the understanding to know what that particular thing is. To interpret, means that you are able by the spirit, to explain or know something thoroughly. However, in order to know the meaning of a thing, you must first understand thing! That's why these gifts of the spirit function best together. Depending on your operation and administration by the spirit, it will determine how often these gifts will manifest in your life.

The office of the prophet will have these gifts in full manifestation more frequently and it will flow more strongly. However, each and every prophet must be trained in this area of the spirit before this operation of administration can become fully functional. No one is exempt from the process nor exempt from training by the means of tests, trials and errors. It happens, and that's why we have a father that overflows with grace!

WISDOM APPLIED

Let's apply the word of Wisdom taken from Proverbs 8 (NLT) and gain a greater understanding of it.

1. Verse 1. Listen as Wisdom calls out! Hear as understanding raises her voice!
• Wisdom cries out for us to hear its voice and to listen, open our ears towards the direction she calls.

2. Verse 2. On the hilltop along the road, she takes her stand at the crossroads.
• The crossroads symbolize the decisions that need to be made in our life. Wisdom stands in the high place, with God, awaiting for us to answer her call before we make a decision.

3. Verses 3-8. By the gates at the entrance to the town, on the road leading in, she cries aloud,

"I call to you, to all of you! I raise my voice to all people. You simple people, use good judgment.

You foolish people, show some understanding. Listen to me!

For I have important things to tell you. Everything I say is right, for I speak the truth and detest every kind of deception. There is nothing devious or crooked in it.

• If you carry God's true wisdom, then nothing
devious should be hiding behind your decisions
You will not make crooked ones to manipulate
another person or way. God's wisdom
is pure, as well as the motives.

4. Verse 9. My words are plain to anyone with
understanding, clear to those with knowledge.
• Here is the words wisdom and knowledge
again. As you can see from the word of God,
these gifts function in operation together.

5. Verse 12. I know where to discover knowledge and discernment.
• The definition of discernment is wisdom.

The definition of wisdom in Hebrew means a skill
So, wisdom is a skill learned of a special kind of craft. To discern a thing is to have the wisdom of a thing. Discernment is not a judge of character, about

a person, however, discernment is to know the motive
of operation, intention, or an ability to obtain spiritual
direction and understanding.

According to the Strong's Concordance, wisdom
can be defined in various ways:

Wisdom (02451) (chokmah [word study] from the
verb chakam - to be wise) is the ability to judge cor-
rectly and to follow the best course of action, based on
knowledge and understanding. Wisdom is the ability
to see something from God's viewpoint. Wisdom is
"God's character in the many practical affairs of life."
Chokmah is the knowledge and the ability to make the
right choices at the opportune time. The consistency
of making the right choice is an indication of one's
spiritual maturity. The prerequisite for this "wisdom"
is the fear of the Lord. "Wisdom" is personified as
crying out for disciples who will do everything to
pursue her. The person who seeks chokmah diligently
will receive understanding: and will benefit in life by
walking with God (Gal 5:16). Chokmah is used most
often in Proverbs, so that the reader of the "wise say-
ings" might know wisdom and allow the Truth of God
to govern his or her life. It follows that it behooves
every child of God to meditate frequently and deeply
on the Words of Wisdom.

Strong's Concordance Chokmah: Wisdom חָכְמָה
:Word Original Part of Speech: Noun Feminine
Transliteration: Chokmah Phonetic Spelling: (khok-maw') Short Definition: Wisdom **Wisdom and un-derstanding is comparable to having discernment**
NAS Exhaustive Concordance Word Origin, from
chakam, Definition, wisdom, NASB Translation

skill (5), skill* (1), wisdom (143), wisely (3),
wits' (1).

CHAPTER 8

DREAMS/MEMORIES
AND THE BRAIN

"There are a hundred billion cells in the human brain all working together!" There are a hundred billion cells in the human brain all working together !Please reference the passage I wrote in my journal about the human brain. Visions are actually happening or what will actually happen (could be inner-eyes closed or eyes open-outer) Both of which contain a prophetic message.

Let's take a look a look at a common issue when it comes to dreams and that is the memory. Before the lord allowed me to interpret dreams, I spent years in heavy research regarding dreams, the brain and the way it shares and stores memories. The brain's consolidation process is imperative when it comes to memories, dreams and visions. Consolidation is the processes of stabilizing a memory trace after the initial acquisition. It may perhaps be thought of part of the process of encoding or of storage, or it may be considered as a memory process in its own right. It is usually considered to consist of two specific processes, synaptic consolidation (which occurs within the first few hours after learning or encoding) and system consolidation (where hippocampus-dependent memories become independent of the hippocampus over a period of weeks to years). (The Human Memory, Memory consolidation, 2010 Lake).

After consolidation, long-term memories are stored throughout the brain as groups of neurons that are primed to fire together in the same pattern that created the original experience and each component of a memory is stored in the brain area that initialized it. (ex; groups of neurons in the visual cortex a sight and the neurons in the amygdala store the associated emotion) Indeed, they may be encoded redundantly, several times, in various parts of the cortex, so that, if one engram or memory trace, is wiped out, there are duplicates or alternative pathways, elsewhere through which the memory may still be retrieved.

In other words, our brains keep copies of memories. The brain stores the sight of the memory as well as the emotion and therefore, it's possible to have one without the other. You can remember, the feeling or emotion of that memory if the actual picture of gets erased. This often times is seen in traumatic situation or events or someone that suffered traumatic brain injuries. Let's look at a scripture that I believe is critical in relation to this research;

Romans 12:2(NLT) Don't copy the behavior and customs of this world, but let God transform you into a new person by changing the way you think. Then you will learn to know God's will for you, which is pleasing and perfect.

Our minds must be transformed by the renewal of our minds in the word of God. We have to imbed the truths of the word into our daily lives because the creator of our brains neurological pathways knew that life would bring trauma, fears, worries and defeat. However, the word of God transforms our thinking thus enabling us to see and discern his will which is "good, acceptable and perfect". How can we know what the will of God is if we are not reading and studying the scriptures? This scripture is also true as believers go through deliverance. Whenever we go through deliverance and demons are cast out of our soul, which is the mind/brain/will and the emotions, which I explained earlier are stored in the amygdala, then we need to retrain our brains to think as God thinks and to discern what is the will of God. You see after deliverance, we are swept clean and become empty vessels waiting to be filled with the word of God. Luke 11:24 NLT, explains very clearly, when an evil spirit leaves a person, it goes into the desert searching for rest. But when it finds none, it says I will return back to the person I came from. When it arrives, it finds the house swept clean and put in order". Please note that the bible references symbolically, that we are a "house". That's why when we dream about houses it represents, "us!"

This scripture denotes that after deliverance our vessel is swept clean. Therefore, we need the word of God or else we become in even worse condition than we previously began. Which leads me to Ephesians 4:23 (NLT): Instead, let the spirit renew your thoughts and attitudes.

Our memories must be actively reconstructed from the elements scattered throughout the brain by the encoding processes. Memory storage is an ongoing process of reclassification resulting from continuous changes in our own neural pathways. (The Human Memory, Memory consolidation, 2010 Lake).

The realm of dreams, visions, and numbers is much heavier than just a mere interpretation, however, it is imperative that we understand the mind/ brain, and nature of our own being and also that our "mind is renewed in the word of God", otherwise we would travel into illegal realms God has not allowed us access!

SLEEP CYCLES

SWS (Known as SLOW WAVE SLEEP)

Bursts of neurological chatter take place during this phase of sleep. However, during this phase, is a period of deep dreamless sleep. It turns out that during this Slow-Wave sleep, there are these episodes where a lot of the cells in the hippocampus will all fire very close to the same time, says wierzynski. (The Human Memory, Memory consolidation, 2010 Lake).

REM SLEEP (Rapid Eye Movement)

According to the California Institute of Technology, REM Sleep is the phase in which dreaming occurs. The previously chatty neuron pairs seemed to talk right past each other, firing at the same rates as before but no longer in concert. The timing relationship almost completely went away during REM SLEEP. *Memories aren't consolidated during this phase of sleep according the thousands of neurological studies. **

This research brings us to the scripture:

Job 33:14-17

For God speaks again and again, though people do not recognize it. He speaks in dreams, in visions of the night, when deep sleep falls on people as they lie in their beds. He whispers in their ears and terrifies them with warnings. He makes them turn from doing wrong, he keeps them from pride.

SLEEP PARALYSIS

What is sleep paralysis? Sleep paralysis is a feeling of being conscious but unable to move. It occurs when a person passes between stages of wakefulness and sleep. During these transitions, you may be unable to move or speak for a few seconds up to a few minutes. Every person that sleeps, passes about 5 phases of sleep per sleep cycle. As we go through these stages of sleep, our body must be able to come out of it. Sleep paralysis occurs when the body has trouble making these transitions. Let's look at two different types of sleep paralysis: Hypnagogic sleep paralysis (predormital), and Hypnopompic (postdormital). (Sleep Paralysis,WebMD,© 2005 - 2018 WebMD LLC, https://www.webmd.com/sleep-disorders/guide/sleep-paralysis#1)

Hypnagogic Sleep Paralysis: Happens when you're falling asleep

Hypnopompic Sleep paralysis: Occurs during waking.

Scientists have also concluded that this is more common among young adults and people with a history of mental illness. A Penn State study found the highest prevalence rates were in students and psychiatric patients. Research has consistently shown that the less sleep you get, the more exhausted you are, therefore the more likely you are to experience sleep paralysis and other sleep disorders. Furthermore, this is a sign that your body is not moving properly through the stages of sleep.

Mental Illness is a terminology that refers to a wide range of mental health conditions that affect your mood, thinking, and behavior. A specific kind of mental illness many people unknowingly suffer from would be Schizophrenia. Greek Origin: Skhizein; meaning split, Greek origin: Phren; mind. Schizophrenia: Which is a breakdown in the relation between thought, emotion, and behavior leading to a faulty perception, withdrawal, and mental fragmentation. The bible speaks about double-minded which is an unstable mind, inappropriate actions or feelings, and disturbances in thought. According to Merriam-Webster. Schizophrenia is a disorder of the mind, and the bible states very clearly that a double minded man is unstable in all his ways James 1:8. This is why the scriptures continuously speak about our MINDS NEEDING TO BE RENEWED in the word of God. God knew what he was doing when he said that and he said it for our own literal health!

That's why it is so very imperative for even our minds to be submitted to God and our very thought life needs to be concentrated on things that are noble, whatever is right, whatever is pure, whatever is lovely, and whatever is admirable. – Philippians 4:8.

CHAPTER 9

THE PROPHETIC REALM OF NUMBER INTERPRETATION

TIMES SEASONS AND PROPHETIC CYCLES

In order to know what the season is come to bring, we must understand the timing. if you can't determine the time of a season, then you won't get to know what the season is. sounds confusing? it's because time and season is related, they're correlated with each other and can't be mentioned without understanding the other. they're identical twins but two different things, makes sense?

Here's some scripture to look into the very timing and seasons of which god operates;

Daniel 2:20-21 King James Version (KJV)

20 Daniel answered and said, Blessed be the name of God for ever and ever: wisdom and might are his: 21 And he changeth the times and the seasons: he removeth kings, and setteth up kings: he giveth wisdom unto the wise, and knowledge to them that know understanding:

Ecclesiastes 1:9 New International Version (NIV)

9 What has been will be again. what has been done will be done again;there is nothing new under the sun.

The scriptures above, describe the times and season in which things happen. these scriptures are the perfect backdrop describing how the lord tends to respond within our natural realm of time, space and matter. how the lord responds are always in prophecies. Prophecies are always linked with prophetic numbers. Numbers are very significant as it relates to prophetic cycles, timing and seasons. When a prophecy is about to be fulfilled numbers will begin to surface and seem more apparent to some. these numbers begin to match and be added to equal certain significant dates and times in history. When we are not in a prophetic cycle the numbers won't make sense!

Please understand that god's timing is not a straight line, (beginning, middle, and end) contrary to what some people believe. God's timing is cyclical.

that means, it repeats in cycles. the bible is literally filled with cyclical patterns of significant events and times. the israelites crossing the jordan river, is the same scene, where Elijah the Prophet is taken up into heaven, then later, jesus is baptized. There are some pretty significant numbers in biblical history that i want to walk you through. the numbers are 40 and the number 120. These 2 numbers are extremely important to pay close attention when it comes to the time table of recording significant dates in history.

Moses spends 40 years in the wilderness as a shepherd in Midian — Exodus 2:11.

The Israelites spends 40 years in the wilderness story begins — Exodus 14

The israelites crossed the jordan river 40 years later into the land of canaan.— Joshua 3

40+40+40=120

120 years represents a prophetic time of fulfillment! Later in Acts 1:15 it states:

"During this time, when about 120 believers were together in one place, peter stood up and addressed them. 16 "Brothers", he said, "the scriptures had to be fulfilled concerning Judas, who guided those who arrested Jesus. this was predicted long ago through king David.

CHAPTER 10

PROPHETIC WORD FOR 2019 USING THE NUMBERS

I released a prophetic word for the year of 2019 on March 14th

Prophetic word for 2019 using the numbers 22, 444, 555, 1212, 1313.

I've been seeing an increase of these numbers more frequently since the turn of this new year. As I was taking notes on our Presidents of the Union speech this is what the Lord spoke to me;Trump's state of the union speech, "as we begin a new Congress and achieve a historic breakthrough, governing not as two parties but as one nation. Victory is not winning for our party victory is winning for our country!

In 2019, we celebrate 50 years since the air pilots flew through space to plant the American flag on the moon (buzz aldrin). We must create a new standard of living. "The First Step Act" congresses criminal Justice reform bill was passed by Congress and signed December 2018 (this act was actually signed in the year of 5779 on the Jewish calendar and in the Jewish month of Kislev which on our Gregorian calendar falls in the month of December) gives non violent offenders an attempt or chance to act to reenter society.

Let's look at the number 9 very quickly, Tet is the ninth number of the Hebrew alphabet. The letter tet is shaped like a vessel, that contains something good that hides it within. This letter is shaped like a womb. This is related to spiritual birthing and nine represents the nine months of pregnancy, where the fetus is hidden within and you cannot see the fetus until the birthing begins to take place. NIne also means goodness and righteousness, fullness, the nine gifts of the spirit. Therefore meaning fullness of the spirit, the full manifestation of the spirit.

THE NUMBER 23 AND THE NUMBERS 22

King Cyrus in the bible is said to be called "king Cyrus the great", his name is mentioned 23 times in the scripture. In the first year of his reign he was prompted by God to decree that the Temple in Jerusalem should be rebuilt and that such Jews as cared might return to their land for this purpose. A significant date in history that confirms this prophetic cycle of fulfilled prophecy would be December 6, 2017. During the first year of President Donald Trump's reign as president he declared formally recognized Jerusalem as the capital of Israel and stated that the American embassy would be moved from Tel Aviv to Jerusalem.

The Jerusalem Embassy Act of 1995 is a public law of the United States passed by the post-Republican Revolution 104th Congress on October 23, 1995. The proposed law was adopted by the Senate (93–5), and the House (374–37). The Act became law without a presidential signature on November 8, 1995.

The time between these significant dates is 22 years.

In 2019 the Lord showed me a vision and in this vision he was looking over governmental documents, old constitutional laws with a magnifying glass. The Lord says there has been old issues that haven't been looked at in years or decades. For too long the Lord says that we've been putting a band-aid over the open wounds of our country, over our neighborhoods and the issues within our communities and the Lord says now I am causing a manifestation of devastation to provoke our government to take a second look at these laws. The lord says that there will be a second look at roe vs Wade and the laws supporting abortions. The lord says that has been a stalemate, meaning difficulty passing laws that satisfy the needs of the body of Christ. And here is what the lord says concerning this:

I've put a certain man in office over the nation of America and This is what the Lord says: "I will go before him and level the mountains. I will smash down gates of bronze and cut through bars of iron. And I will him treasures hidden in the darkness— secret riches. I will do this so all may know that I am the Lord , the God of Israel, the one who has called him by name. "And why have I called him for this work? Why did I call him by name when he did not know me? It is for the sake of Jacob my servant, Israel my chosen one. I am the Lord ; there is no other God. I have equipped him for battle, though he didn't even know me, so all the world from east to west will know there is no other God. I am the Lord, and there is no other.— Isaiah 45:2-6 NLT

1212 APOSTOLIC REFORMATION

1. Apostolic Age of Reformation.

To reform means to make changes to something with the intention of setting it back on the right path. God is making changes now to the DNA of the Apostles and Prophets who are pure, prophetic, and peculiar. We will be seeing a rising of apostolic teachers of the fivefold and Apostles with a strong teaching dimension. Apostolic theologians will bring clarity and understanding to the scripture, who will stand as Paul stood with power and demonstration of the spirit, preaching persuasively to win souls for the kingdom of God.

2. Apostolic Teams

I see teams being sent out 2 by 2, witnessing the gospel to others in various regions and territories. Teams of 2 organizing and managing. A Rise of Apostolic Hubs, Businesses And kingdom Assignment This era we are in denotes a time of maturity in the body of Christ. This is not a time to be weak or crippled by fear. However, it's a time to know your identity in Christ Jesus. I see new levels of organization and management coming to the Ecclesia where there was confusion and chaos.

This is a result of the rising teachers, apostolic theologians, kingdom businesses and hubs. There will be much equipping in 2018 for the Ecclesia. From 2018 and on, you'll see an increase of prophets and apostles in business dominating the entrepreneurial game; prophets who are masters in ecommerce, trading, and stocks. Organizational prophets and apostles obtaining high positions in secular companies reigning as Daniel reigned in King Nebuchadnezzar's royal court and the Spirit of the Lord will be heavily upon them. Don't despise working in a secular market or working among unbelievers in this era because the Spirit of the Lord will be with you as you release the light of Christ. Ordinary Churches operating without the spirit of God will die out quickly in this era, and the pastoral model will crumble if it's not led by a pastor that carries "apostolic DNA".

3. Age of the Apostles or Acts of the Apostles

I love how the book of Acts opens, making reference of how close the apostles were to Christ. After his death, he appeared to them on numerous times. He proved to them in many ways that he was actually alive (Acts 1 verse 3). In Acts 2, you see and read that the Holy Spirit came suddenly and there was a sound from heaven like a roaring of a mighty windstorm and it filled the house where they were sitting (Acts 2:2). God has shown me how He will drench His holy apostles and prophets in this new era and the power of the Spirit of the living God will be upon their lives so heavy.

I remember as I slept one night, I had a dream and in this dream, I saw Jesus commissioning a small group of apostles. He was preparing them to be sent out, and before He sent them out, He gave them a book to read from. It was an oath taken from the Gospel of Matthew 10:16 that these Apostles took. I remember looking down at the book in my hand and seeing the letters in that book, and the letters were glowing. I remember reciting the words as the other apostles were and shortly after, my eyes opened. I believe the Lord was showing me that there is a remnant of apostles that will carry real healing, real power, and possess true authority from the Father. The Holy Spirit explained that He is commissioning a remnant that was the point of the group being "small". Also, note the writing that glowed. The Lord revealed that His word shall be amplified through the mouths of these remnants. The oaths they took were to mean a promise to stand and live by the words of God in order to fulfill His plans on earth.

The Lord is re-establishing the order at the border. Many children will be rejoined with their families, that have been separated. The families and the people that are already there at the border will be issued a temporary citizenship card literally issued to each and every person, but they have to pass a clearance, customs, and thorough background checks.

I have raised up a Joshua generation which has the mindset of conquering! Rising of entrepreneurs a generation of soulpreneurs, spiritual entrepreneurs, kingdomprenuers these are the remnants God has chosen to re-establish the order of the marketplace within the sphere of business and ecommerce.

God is canceling debt supernaturally. 222 and 555 represent expansion and multiplication of our nation. The Bible refers to Cyrus as the one who saved the Jews being known as Cyrus the great. During his reign, he expanded the kingdom. I believe this is another prophetic cycle being repeated from the reign of king cyrus to to the presidency of Donald Trump.

The president's record of expansion

1. Almost 4 million jobs created since the election
2. More Americans are now employed than ever recorded before in our history.
3. We have created more than 400,000 manufacturing jobs since my election.
4. manufacturing jobs growing at the fastest rate in more than THREE DECADES.
5. Economic growth last quarter hit 4.2 percent.

The above is just a small example of the growth and expansion under the presidency of Trump, it shouldn't matter how we feel about a certain person, as long as the country moves in the direction it needs to go according to what the lord wants to do! not our will, but his will be done on earth, as it is in heaven!

Numbers have such a profound meaning to our lives than many believers fail to realize or acknowledge. Many people are not awakened to this particular realm of the spirit and how number interpretation can impact a prophetic message to a believer. Often times, numbers are codes, hidden within a specific message waiting to be unlocked. Like dreams, the realm of interpreting numbers is shared within the revelatory realm of information stated in 1 Corinthians 12:8 KJV.

The bible clearly states there are diversities of operations, but it is the same God that worketh all in all (1 Cor 12:6 KJV) This means that it is by the spirit who gives us the diversities of gifting's, but it is one God that does it all. The spirit allows the manifestation of that particular gifting to operate so that the body of Christ can prosper. You see here in scripture, it clearly states, that the revelatory realm of the spirit is given so that we may benefit. Let's look at the operation of the revelatory realm and how it manifests. In 1 Cor 12:8, it says, "For one is given by the spirit the word of wisdom; to another the word of knowledge by the same spirit". Although the spirit will allow these two operations to work by itself or stand on its own through any believer he chooses, the word of wisdom and the word of knowledge works together to open up the realm of revelation.

This realm is meant to unlock, decode, breakdown, reveal, expose and unveil the very messages the lord is saying for you, for your church, for your region or for your nation. I also want to make very clear the working of the gift of prophecy in connection to these two spiritual gifts. (1 Cor 12:10 KJV) Therefore, if you can access this realm of the spirit, you would have a heavy ability, by the spirit of course, of three gifts manifesting and working together all at once for the good or profit of whoever is receiving ministry.

I have interpreted countless of numbers for people that didn't give me any information beforehand, but the numbers they were seeing. Often times, I've never seen these people, I have never met them, however, it is the spirit of God who knows every hair on their head, it is God who knows even when they sit down or stand up, the lord knows your thoughts even when your far away. The lord knows everything you do. The bible says that such knowledge is to wonderful for us, and to great to understand. We can never escape the lord's spirit! (Psalm 139:1-6).

Many people in the body of Christ have only scratched the surface of number meaning, their interpretation and how to properly minister to someone through number interpretation. Repeating numbers or seeing multiples of the same numbers, only means that the single meaning of that number has tripled in meaning and now takes upon a heavier, weighty spiritual significance. This is known as the Triad affect. Often times, people will see groups or three pairs of the same numbers in a row. For example; 333, 111, 222, 444, 555, 777, 888, 10.10, 12.12, 11.11....etc.

Triad Affect is a group or set of three connected numbers, it also denotes that it will affect 3 areas of your life.

CHAPTER 11

NUMBER INTERPRETATION AND THE GEMATRIA COMBINED

111 (IF YOU'RE SEEING MULTIPLES OF THIS NUMBER)

I believe this number holds a heavy spiritual significance to our personal lives and to our world around us. This teaching wouldn't be right if I didn't begin with Genesis 1:1-5 In the beginning God created the heavens and the earth. The earth was formless and empty, and darkness covered the deep waters. And the Spirit of God was hovering over the surface of the waters. Then God said, "Let there be light," and there was light. And God saw that the light was good. Then he separated the light from the darkness. God called the light "day" and the darkness "night." And evening passed and morning came, marking the first day.

The number 111 speaks about setting and commanding things into order, into alignment, shifting things into place. God is commanding order and calling the light to shine through you.

Prophetic message: I can't help but to see the valley of the dry bones in Ezekiel 37. I hear the spirit of the lord say, "I am commanding dry bones to be refreshed!"

The apostolic mandate draws you to himself (Christ). It separates you from the world. This number also signifies the new beginning, fresh start in 3 areas of your life. It denotes a new beginning and fresh start because of what God did in the book of Genesis. He created, he commanded the world, separating the light from the dark. So, in our lives, the lord God, separates his truth from the false, separating the chaff from the wheat, his word divides joint and marrow, soul and spirit!

The number 1 also signifies unity. Ephesians 4:5 There is One Lord, one faith, one baptism. One God and father of all, who is over all, in all, and living through all.

A-Aleph-

each hebrew letter actually used to be accompanied with a pictograph, similar to hieroglyphics. the original pictograph related to this picture is actually an ox, or what looks similar to one.

ox/strength/leader/father

apostolic- 1st in command and represents a strong leader. this pictograph relates to the apostolic grace and the the apostolic anointing. this means that it points to the leader or the father. a husband/father is the head of the wife, but christ is the head of the husband and the church.

222 (IF YOU'RE SEEING MULTIPLES OF THIS NUMBER

By itself this number represents either:
1. union
2. division

3. witnessing
4. Multiplication
5. Expansion
6. Verification/Confirmation;

you definitely want to keep in mind that when you are seeing this number, the Holy Spirit wants to confirm a message that he has told you of what will soon take place or has taken place. However, whenever the number is seen in a series like this, it can mean a combination of all these things

Genesis 1:6-7 (NLT) Then God said, "Let there be a space between the waters, to separate the waters of the heavens from the waters of the earth." 7 And that is what happened. God made this space to separate the waters of the earth from the waters of the heavens.

Adam and Eve, Husband and wife=Union
Witnessing 2 Cor 13:1 This is the third time I am coming to you. In the mouth of two or three witnesses shall every word be established.

I've noticed in the scriptures, their were always 2 traveling together in pairs, by two's doing missionary work, God's work, speaking and often preaching together. For example, Paul & Silas, Barnabas & James, Paul & Barnabas, Junia & Adronicas. Elijah & Elisha, Luke 10:1 states that Jesus sent out the apostles by 2's. The bible even states that two are better than one.

bet/vet- pronounced "bait", rhymes with mate, date

this is the second letter of the hebrew alph-bet (alef-beyt), with an original pictograph of a house, meaning to dwell in or live in.

1. the idea of house is a very basic idea on 3 realms of the spiritman.
2. the house level-the natural realm
3. the soul level-the soulish man

The heavenly/or the spirit- this is housed with god seated in heavenly places. psalms 92:13 those that be planted in the house of the lord shall flourish in the courts of our god.the torah actually begins with bet. the letter bet connotes power because of the force of air being spoken forth. god's ruach/spirit.

333 (IF YOU'RE SEEING MULTIPLES OF THIS NUMBER)

1.   God calling your attention to a particular area

A.   God calls Samuel 3 times (three times to get his attention) 1 Samuel 3:4-1

B.   2 Cor 13:1 This is the third time I am coming to you

C.   Paul preaches in the synagogues for three months and argues persuasively about the kingdom of God Acts 19:8

This number also represents Christ. The scriptures reveal that this number symbolizes vegetation, seed-bearing fruit- meaning that you are carrying around something that can be given to someone else; as in a spiritual birthing that can take place. Genesis 1:11 These-seeds will then produce the kinds of plants and trees from which they came.

3 also represents the spirit of Christ Being released

Mark 15:25 It was nine o'clock in the morning when they crucified him. From the 6am-9am=3 hours. 7=1, 8=2, 9=3. Jesus was crucified on the cross in the 3rd hour according to the amplified version or translation of scripture. (9am)

The spirit of Christ was released in Mark 15:37 because he gave his last breath. Jesus rose on the third day.

3 also represents the resurrection, this emphasis is on the Power of the God's spirit that was released into the earth to raise Christ from the dead because Christ was in the earth!!

That's why it is so imperative to pay close attention to what God is saying especially concerning the Triad affects. I have heard some people saying that numbers or seeing triple numbers are non-sense or the use of interpreting numbers are not necessary. I must disagree. The lord speaks in so many different ways through his creation as he chooses, but only if we be open to his various avenues of speaking. What we must understand is that the lord will go to great lengths to get our attention. However, if we are not awakened to this we will miss the very message, or call the lord is conveying. We cannot close ourselves off to his glory and say the avenues of which he speaks are nonsense because of ignorance.

The promises of God
A promise is a declaration or assurance that something will be done.

The number 33 is connected to a promise or the promises of God. The 33rd time Noah's name is mentioned in the bible, God promises never to destroy the entire world again with a flood and seals his pledge with the sign of the rainbow (Genesis 9:12-16).

This number refers to a solemn promise or oath from you made to god, that god remembers you made. the account of scripture we can reference for this would be when jacob's name is mentioned for the 33rd time in scripture he made a promise to the lord to give a tenth of all he had to god when he had the vision of a ladder reaching to heaven (Genesis 28:10 - 12, 16 - 22). this number can also denote that the lord is taking a look at your financial health and stability as a giver.

Since 33 is the product of 11, and 11 means transitions or judgement, it can possibly mean god's final judgment or a transitioning away from god's judgement or wrath.

g-gimmel-pronounced geeh-mel and has a g sound like "g" in grill

the early pictograph for this letter is foot/camel

the letter represents the both giving and returning. running and returning, reward and punishment. every action is stored and remembered and the person must give an account for every action they've done. another aspect of the gimmel is that it equals 3. there is an emphasis of dimension made here.. this letter says that there is three levels of reality, or harmony. the star of david is represented of three triangles. in other words this number represents the balance of things.

444 (IF YOU'RE SEEING MULTIPLES OF THIS NUMBER)

The number 4 relates to the preaching of the gospel to the ends of the earth. as the water covers the sea. being broken before the lord in order to spread the good news of Jesus Christ. Prophets, seers, apostles, dreamers and visionaries are more likely to see this series of 4's because they are being broken before the lord, in order for God's mission to achieved.

*Denotes creative works; the number of creation; God completed the material universe on the 4th day. He brought into existence our sun, moon, and all the stars. Their purpose was hot only to give off light, but also, to divide the day from the night, thus becoming a basic demarcation of time. In essence the number 4 equates to the world around us, the earth, the seasons and times, the anointing of Issachar as it relates to knowing what season the body of Christ is in, even for your own life. The Hebrew word for seasons is Moed (Strong's concordance #4150), which is literally translated to mean 'appointed times'(divine appointments).

In Ezekiel 1:5, we notice 4 Cherubim's are introduced as living beings that looked human. I will break this creature down in another chapter, however, I will state that this Cherubim is symbolic for the earth, and movement throughout the earth. Also, represents, The dominions and rulership of those upon the earth and the four corners of the earth.

Acts 12:4 Then he imprisoned him, placing him under the guard of FOUR squads of soldiers each. This also gives the point of reference to being covered on every side. Like the four corners of the earth.

The four witnesses of God on earth are miracles, signs, wonders, and the gifts of the Holy Spirit see Hebrews 2:4. Therefore, the number 4 is speaking to us concerning times and seasons for specific movements to come in the earth. God's spirit performing signs, wonders and miracles covering the earth and the movement throughout it as the gospel is preached.

the fourth letter of the hebrew alph-bet (alef-beyt) is dalet pronounced "dah-let" and has the sound of "d" as in david or delta.

the early pictograph of this letter is said to be of a door/tent (a poor person) or state of humbleness or lowly position a greatest of positions or pathway/entryway. a true relationship or intimacy with god is of a humble position.

the shape of the dalet says that it is of self nullification. there is a little point on the right that sticks out and it is the point of ego. we all have an ego even within a humble person. however, when our ego is left unchecked, it may get out of hand, resulting in rebellion. the doorway to true spiritual service is called nullification of the ego. in relationship to god, the whole creation is in a state of humbleness, in which creation bows to him.

555 IF YOU'RE SEEING MULTIPLES OF THIS NUMBER

This number by itself is said to mean "Grace". According to Genesis 1:22, on the 5th day God says, be fruitful and multiply let the fish fill the seas and let the birds multiply on the earth. This verse is key because not only does this number mean grace, however, it's associated with multiplication. Let's further explore the reason of the five being "multiplication. In Matthew 14:13-21 we notice that Jesus feeds the five thousand. A closer look reveals the instruction Jesus gave to his disciples; Jesus replied, "They do not need to go away. You give them something to eat." "We have here only five loaves of bread and two fish," they answered. This denotes that the number 2 also is associated with multiplication. Then it goes on to say, Jesus took the five loaves and two fish, looked up toward heaven, and blessed them. What happened in these versus, is called a 'Prophetic act'. Jesus performed an act of provision, which would have a powerful manifestation in the natural of gaining supernatural provision.

Praying over your finances or food is not just something you do, but it means you are partnering with the father to provide more of what you have by allowing him to multiply it 2x over!! Therefore, 5 is the number of Grace, provision, and multiplication. Can I take this just a but further?? Why am I asking? You know I will!

This number is also associated with God's glory and his anointing oil. God's glory is found in Exodus 26-27 as it describes the tabernacle in the wilderness. In exodus 25:8 god instructs the israelites to make a sanctuary for me, and I will dwell among them. When God's presence shows up, it appears as a glory cloud. Within god's glory cloud are healings, signs, wonders and miracles. IN exodus 30:23-25 we see the ingredients for the holy anointing oil. The ingredients were directly given by God and contained five ingredients directly given by God which wee;myrrh, sweet cinnamon, sweet calamus and cassia.

the fifth letter of the hebrew alph-bet (alef-beyt) and pronounced "hey" and has the sound of "h" as in "hay".

this letter is constructed from a dalet and a foot. the gimmel which means to give, gives as if it were apart of the foot to dalet, the poor person. which in turn becomes the "hey" this letter symbolizes a unity and completeness. it stands for expression and revelation.

the sixth letter of the hebrew alph-bet (alef-beyt) is called "vav", shaped like a vertical line, is a very significant letter, as it has an early pictograph of a man standing connecting heaven to earth, it represents the idea of connection to those 3 realms, it spiritually connecting heaven and earth, similar to that of jacob's ladder. the first time the letter appears in torah, appears its the central headquarters of the word or letter, in the first verse of the torah. "in the beginning god created heaven and earth". the vav is connecting heaven and earth. this tell us the role of the vav, from the practical to the mystical, its connecting everything in the universe. in the first word of the torah, there are six letters and it is further manifest in the account of creation which takes places in six days. so the idea of six represents all of creation.

THE CYCLES OF SIX

this letter sets the scene for all the cycles of history.

6000 years would pass before the coming of the messiah

man works for six days

man was created on the sixth day

six years we work our fields and on the seventh we rest

777 (SEEING MULTIPLES OF THIS NUMBER 777)

The number 7 by itself denotes the hallmark of the holy Spirit's work

The number 7 has 7 symbolic meanings in scripture;

1.   Completeness; Philippians 1:6 being confident of this that he who began a good work in you will carry it on to completion

2.   Fullness

3.   Perfection

4.   To swear

5.   To Vow

6.   To make an oath. **Jacob bowed 7 times to the ground when he saw his brother Esau Gen 33. This signified an oath and vow he made to his brother Esau. **

7. It also means rest since earth was completed on the 7th day.

As you can see, this number by itself is very simple to interpret, however, when it relates to a triad of the numbers 777 it could be any combination of these symbolic meanings. However, it would depend greatly upon the individual rand the message the holy spirit speaks to you in regards to the prophetic ministry through that number.

Here is an example of a number interpretation request I received from someone regarding the number 7.

Number Interpretation

"Blessings to you WOG. I'm growing in the spirit with God seeking his face day by day fighting the flesh with the holy spirit. However, I always encountered the number 7. I was the 7th person to walk across the stage during graduation in 2015. I did a scratch off that is attached and 777 where on there also. I just took a test for the postal service. My results were 77.7. I look forward to chatting or speaking with you..."

Interpretation:

Hello Man of God! Wow, as soon as I read this the Lord instantly spoke to me regarding what you wrote to me and this is what the Lord says, "Since birth, I've marked you. Marked you for greatness to pursue the destiny, I the Lord has placed in your heart. I am perfecting you and perfecting the areas of your life Business, finances, and ministry. I've called you to the marketplace in business to spread the Gospel in various places and to people who do not know me. My perfection is upon you my son. I am daily loading you with benefits as you draw unto me in prayer and as you abide in me in the secret place, I am abiding in you. My son, I am blessing the work of your hands so that you may fulfill every good work I send you to." The Lord also showed me that you are getting and will be working for the postal service so your career there will be steady.

Abundant Blessings!

His response:
"Glory to God! How accurate!!! I knew it! Yes! Hallelujah. I shout for Joy...Thank you Lord God ..My mom Gave me up to God when I was first born...I'm being patience and allowing God to abide in me. God bless you WOG".

In the example above, of a real number interpretation, you see the fluidness of the gift of prophecy,

word of knowledge and the word of wisdom working together to provide a clear and accurate message
straight from the father's heart.

The seventh letter of the hebrew alph-bet (alef-
beyt) is called zayin pronounced "zah-yeen" and has
the sound of "z" like zebra. the pictograph for zayin
looks like a sword.

The root meaning of the Hebrew letter Zayin is in-
teresting in itself. While it means a "sword "or "sharp
weapon", as explained above, the meaning of the word
is also connected to food and sustenance. For example, the Modern Hebrew word "mazon" (וזמ), meaning "food" or "sustenance", and the Modern Hebrew
word "hazana" (הנזה), meaning "nourishment", both
come from the same root as Zayin. Some scholars say
that the meaning behind this is that while pointless
bloodshed is certainly not the ideal, we sometimes
must fight in order to defend our lives and our way
of life.

Just as its literal meaning is complex, the spiritual meaning of the Hebrew letter Zayin is significant, as well. The letter has the numerical value of seven, which has much significance, including the fact that the Sabbath is the seventh and holiest day of the week, and according to Biblical law, the land is meant to lie fallow every seventh year according to a law called "shmita". As Ziyan is the first letter of the word "zahor" (רוכז), meaning to remember, and this is one of two basic commandments of the Sabbath, there seems to be a very strong link between the seventh letter in the Hebrew alphabet and the day of rest!

888 (IF YOU'RE SEEING MULTIPLES OF THIS NUMBER)

The number 8 has basic significance even when tripled, that has deep spiritual biblical roots dating back to the book of genesis. Abraham the father of faith had 8 sons which symbolized a new beginning in the earth Jesus appeared to his disciples 8 times after he was resurrected and brought to life. The new 8 also signifies the mark of the covenant. —Genesis 17:11-12 NLT

You must cut off the flesh of your foreskin as a sign of the covenant between me and you. From generation to generation, every male child must be circumcised on the eighth day after his birth. This applies not only to members of your family but also to the servants born in your household and the foreign-born servants whom you have purchased.

I have noticed an increase amount of people in the body of Christ seeing the numbers 611, 411, 711, 911 and this is what it means-These numbers relate to the deeper revelatory realm of information, insight, spiritual wisdom, knowledge, and spiritual awakening to the revelatory. God is drawing you deeper into this realm because he desires for you to have a new level of spiritual maturity in this particular area and god's desire is to bring the operation of word of wisdom, word of Knowledge, discerning of spirits and prophecy to full operation and allow them to flow together.

the eighth letter of the hebrew alph-bet (alef-beyt) is pronounced "chet" rhyming with "met or bet."

The Hebrew letter Het is associated with a number of positive character traits. For example, the Hebrew word "hohma" (המכוח), meaning "wisdom" begins with the letter Het, as does the word "hasidut" (תודיסח), which means "righteousness", and "hen" (ןח) meaning "grace". The numerical value of the letter Het is eight, which is often associated with super-spirituality or holiness, as it is one more than seven, which represents the holy realm of the Sabbath. When Jewish boys are circumcised and enter into their faith's holy ancient covenant, it is commanded to be performed on the eighth day.

In connecting with the super-holiness and positive attributes associated with the letter Het, it is also important to note that the letter Het begins the word "hayim" (םייח) meaning life. The letter also looks like a doorway. In thinking about all of this information related to the Hebrew letter Het together, some think that the important message we can learn from the letter is that the way we can pass through the "doorway" to a good life is by instilling in ourselves and in our children good values, such as wisdom, righteousness, and grace!

THE NUMBER 999 (SEEING MULTIPLES OF THIS NUMBER)

This number by itself signifies the fruit of the spirit, divine completion from the father. This number has three significant meanings in scripture:

1. The 9 gifts of the spirit
2. Sevenfold spirit
3. The 9 fruits of the spirit

Those who are particularly seeing the number 999 needs to know this is also in Strong's Concordance.

999=Binah

Binah: An understanding

Phonetic spelling: Bee-Naw

Word of origin: Aramaic corresponding to binah

Daniel 2:21-22 he deposes kings and raises up others. He gives wisdom to the wise and knowledge to the discerning. He reveals deep and hidden things; he knows what lies in darkness, and light dwells with him.

In Hebrew, it's Biynah meaning knowledge. This was Daniel's prayer as he interpreted the dream of the King Nebuchadnezzar's dream. Daniel inquired of the lord and God opened up the realm of revelation and poured it over Daniel.

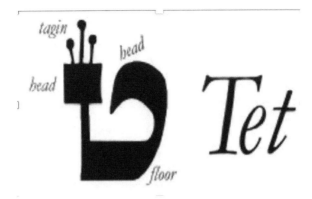

TET: the letter "tet" is shaped like a vessel that contains something good, however, it hides it within. hebrew letter is equivalent to the number 9 in hebrew, which is shaped like a womb. this is related to the spiritual birthing, in which nine is represented by the 9 months of pregnancy where the fetus is hidden within and you cannot see the fetus until the birthing begins to take place.

Nine also means goodness, righteousness, fullness, nine gifts of the spirit, and the nine fruits of the spirit. therefore, meaning, fullness of the spirit. full manifestations of the spirit are taking place in your life!

737- Boeing 737; powerful jet plane; ignitor of souls and hearts, separator of joints and marrow; power of the spirit; carrying the spirit of the lord with authority and reverence.

10 – Journey, wilderness (Pastor); this number also symbolizes a time of testing through trials. the lord is testing your heart, patience and finances.

the letter Yod, (also yud;yodh) is the tenth letter of the hebrew alph-bet (alef-beyt);pronounced "yood" best rhymes with mode. the pictograph of "yod or yud" looks similar to a hand or arm.

This is the first letter of gods name. this letter represents god's concept of his contraction, and that is why this letter may symbolically mean, "the little that holds a lot". where our present universe, people tend to believe that our world came from the big bang, this is where scientists tend to get this theory from. all 22 letters, has a yud in them. in the jewish mystical tradition, yod represents a mere dor, a divine point of energy. since, yod is used to form all the letters, and since god uses the letters as the building blocks of creation, yod indicates god's omnipresence.

Since yeshua upholds the world by the word of his power (hebrew 1:3), and yod is part of every hebrew letter (and therefore every word), yod is considered the starting point of the presence of god in all things- the "spark of the spirit in everything.

Now ten is a number marking shelemut, or completion and order, as evidenced by the following:

- the base 10 number system is universal.
- there were ten things created on the first day and ten things created at the end of the sixth day of creation.
- there were ten generations from adam to noah, suggesting that the godliness of the father of the nations.
- there were ten plagues issued during the exodus of egypt.
- god gave us ten commandments.
- the tenth part shall be holy for the lord (leviticus 27:32)

11 – Transition (Prophet) negative god's judgement/wrath

The eleventh letter of the hebrew alph-bet (alef-beyt) is called "kaf" and has the sound of "k" as in "kite". this letter has the numeric value of 20. the early pictograph for kaf looks similar like a palm of a hand, whereas the classical hebrew script is constructed of a bent line that appears somewhat like a crown on the head of a prostrating king. the word kaf means "palm" of a hand and also what might be contained within the palm of the hand. the word spoon in hebrew is the word kaf, which is a natural extension of the hand as a container. the gematria for the letter kaf is 20, the same value for the word yod (hand), and twice the value of the letter yod.

12 – Government (Apostle)

The twelfth letter of the hebrew aleph-bet (alef-beyt), is called lamed, pronounced lah-med and has the numeric value of 30. the pictograph of lamed looks like a shepherd's staph or goad. The shepherd staff was used to direct sheep by pushing or pulling them. It was also used as a weapon against predators to defend and protect the sheep.

The meaning of this letter is "toward" as moving something in a different direction. This letter also means "authority," as it is a sign of the shepherd, the leader of the flock. It also means "yoke," which is a staff on the shoulders, "tie" or "bind" from idea of the yoke that is bound to the animal.

This letter is used as a prefix to nouns meaning "to" or "toward."

13 – Rebellion

The letter "mem" is the 13th letter of the hebrew aleph-bet (alef-beyt), Symbolizing water (it can also mean chaos (stormy water), mighty, or blood. It's the 13th letter. It is a consonant . It is also the number 40 when used as a number.

The pictograph for MeM looks like a wave of water. in jewish mysticism, the letter mem, is the letter of "water", symbolizing the springs of the torah. just as the waters of an underground spring rise upward from an unknown source to reveal themselves, so does the spring of wisdom rise up from the mysterious source that is god.

14 – Double anointing

15 – Reprieve, mercy

16 – Established beginnings

17 – Election

25 – Begin ministry training

30 – Begin ministry

111 – My Beloved Son

666 – Full lawlessness (depending on how often your seeing this number could represent the lord calling you, a church or organization toward repentance.

888 – Resurrection

10,000 – Maturity

CHAPTER 12

DREAM DICTIONARY

ANIMALS

Alligator/Crocodile- sea monster. Ancient demonic stronghold that is deeply rooted.; represents a demonic stronghold in the bloodline, possible generational, also any reptilian like creature represents leviathan (see Job 41, Isaiah 27:1). If the alligator's mouth is open it represents anger, aggression.

Bat- Represents Witchcraft, fear, soulish.

Bears-of any type- Ancient demonic spirit, strength, opposition, stronghold.

Beaver- Ardent, diligent, clever.

Black Horse – feminine; bad times; evil (Rev 6:5).

Black Panther – high level witchcraft; demonic activity, or works in darkness.

Bull- Anger, aggression.

Cat-unclean spirit, self-willed, demonic spirit;friendly cat means your blind to hidden sin;black cat means witchcraft, hidden agendas, a spirit of fear and superstition.

Cheetah-Swift, fast, spiritual stealth and stamina. On the flip side, could mean danger or a play on words for "Cheater."

Chicken- cowardliness;depending on the tone of the dream and setting. Chickens peck when they eat so it could mean pecking at an issue and not getting to the root or pecking at something and not full aware that it needs to be left alone;fault finding.

Cobras, rattlesnake, - python spirit; seeking to squeeze out your prayer life. fear. Mouth open means venom, spiritual attack, or warfare.

Cow-substance; provision; prosperity.

Crab-spirits of irritation, aggravation and frustration.

Dinosaur- Old stronghold, demonic, danger from the past, generational stronghold, spirit of Leviathan in the bloodline.

Dog-Unbelievers, hypocrites, friendly dogs could mean disloyalty, friendly dogs;someone befriending you who is possibly unfaithful;be sure to keep in mind the tone of the dream and setting.

Donkey- Issachar anointing, gentle strength, stable, on the negative side however, it could mean; stubbornness, hard headed.

Dove-purity, holy spirit.

Eagle- soaring to new heights and new levels in the spirit, prophetic accuracy prophetic anointing and calling.

Elephant- strength, thick skinned; not easily offended, long pregnancy; good stored memory.

Fish-souls; people; colored fish denotes people of different nationalities and ethnicities.

Fox- Cunning.

Frog- hinderance; spirit of lust.

Goat- sin, unbelief, stubborn, argumentative, lacking discernment;play on words or "scapegoat."

Hawk- unclean spirit; predator, sorcerer; evil spirit;witchcraft; these birds are the opposite of the symbolism of an eagle.

Hen – one who gathers; protects.

Horse – Power, strength, conquest; spiritual warfare.

Leopard – swiftness, sometimes associated with vengeance, predator, or danger.

Lion – Jesus "Lion of the tribe of Judah"; royalty,kingship, bravery; confidence; Satan seeking to destroy.

Lobster – not easy to approach.

Mice – something small that bring destruction; devourer, curse, plague, or timid.

Mole – spiritual blindness.

Monkey – foolishness; clinging; mischief; dishonesty; or addiction.

Mountain Lion – Satan, enemy; predator seeking to destroy.

Octopus /squid-Spirits of mind control because of the tentacles that attach to its prey; manipulation, control also, Jezebel. These animals are found in water or deep waters which symbolizes demonic spirits found deeply rooted in the soul- which is the mind, will and emotions, or strongholds.

Ostrich- Unclean spirit.

Owl- witchcraft, unclean spirit/ can also represent wisdom in the non dream state.

Ox – slow change; subsistence.

Pig – ignorance; hypocrisy; religious unbelievers, unclean people; selfish, gluttonous;vicious, or vengeful.

Raccoon – mischief; night raider; rascal; thief, bandit; deceitful.

Ram – sacrifice.

Rat – feeds on garbage or impurities; unclean spirit, or invader.

Raven – evil, Satan.

Red Horse – persecution; anger; danger; opposition (Rev 6:4).

Sea Gull-demonic spiritual scavenger.

Sheep – the people of God; innocent, vulnerable; humility; submission; sacrifice.

Skunk – "stinking up" a situation; unforgiveness, bitterness; or bad attitude.

Sloth – slow moving; easy prey, or vulnerable.

Snake – Satan & evil spirits (pay attention to the colors and type of snake) deception, lies; Satan; unforgiveness, or bitterness;

Sparrow – small value but precious; watched by the Lord.

Tiger – danger; powerful minister (both good & evil), soul power, or demonic spirit.

Tortoise–slow moving; slow change; steady; old; old way of doing something; wise.

Turkey – foolish; clumsy; dumb; thanksgiving.

Vulture – spiritual scavenger;unclean spirit; impure;an evil person;greedy; covetous.

Weasel – wicked; breaking promises (as in "weaseling out of a deal"); informant or tattletale; traitor.

Whale – big impact in the things of the Spirit;deep things of the spirit.

White Horse – salvation; rescue; redeem; royalty.

White Snake – spirit of religion; occult.

Wolf – Agents of Satan and evil; false ministries, false teachers, false prophets, false apostles, false pastors;predatory spirits.

BODY PARTS

Arm – strength; faith.

Bald Head – lacking wisdom.

Beard – maturity.

Fingers 17
• Thumb – apostolic.
• Pointer – prophetic.
• Middle – evangelistic.
• Ring – pastor.
• Pinky – teaching.
Hair – wisdom & anointing(.17)
Hand – relationship; healing.17
Immobilized Body Parts – spiritual hindrance;demonic attack.(17)

Nakedness – Positive: being transparent; humility; innocence. Negative: lust; temptation; in or of the flesh (.17)

Neck – Positive: support or strength. Negative: stiffnecked, or stubborn.17

Nose – discernment.17

Side – relationship; or friendship.17

Teeth – wisdom; comprehension;or understanding.17

Eye Teeth – revelatory understanding. Wisdom Teeth – ability to act in wisdom.

Thigh – faith.17

CLOTHES

Bathrobe – coming out of a place of cleansing.

Clothing that doesn't fit – walking in something you're not called to.

Cultural Clothing – missionary calling; prayer calling for a particular country or ethnic group.

Coat – mantle, anointing.17

Pajamas – spiritual slumber.

Shoes – Gospel of peace.

Shorts – a walk or calling that is partially fulfilled. Speedo – to move fast in the spirit.

Swimwear – ability to move in the Spirit.

Tattered Clothing – mantle or anointing that's not being taken care of.

Wedding Dress – covenant; deep relationship.

COLORS

Black – death, or mystery. Negative – sin, or darkness.

Blue – revelation or communion/ Negative – depression, sorrow, or anxiety.

Brown – compassion, or humility/ Negative – compromise, or humanism.

Gold/amber – purity, glory, or holiness/ Negative – idolatry, defilement, or licentiousness.

Gray – maturity, honor, or wisdom/ Negative – weakness.

Green – growth, prosperity, or conscious/ Negative – envy, jealousy, or pride. Orange – perseverance. Negative – stubbornness.

Pink – childlike, or love of God/ Negative – childishness.

Purple – authority, or royalty/ Negative – false authority

Red – wisdom, anointing, & power/ Negative – anger, or war.

Silver – redemption, or grace/ Negative – legalism.

White – righteousness, or holiness/ Negative – religious spirit.

Yellow – hope, or mind/ Negative – fear, cowards, or intellectual pride.

DIRECTION

Back – Past: (as in backyard or back door). Previous event or experience (good or evil); that which is behind (for example, past sins or the sins of forefathers);unaware, unsuspecting; hidden; memory (Genesis 22:13;Joshua 8:4; Philippians 3:13).

East – Beginning (Genesis 11:2); Law (therefore blessed or cursed);birth;first (sun rises in the east bringing hope and new day); false religions (as in "Eastern religions"). Psalm 103:12 "As far as the east (law) is from the west (grace), so far hath He removed our transgressions from us."

East Wind – judgment, hardship (Genesis 41:23, 27; Exodus 10:13).

Front – Future or Now: (as in front yard or front porch) prophecy of future events; immediate;current Rev.1:19 "Write the things which thou hast seen, and the things which (presently) are (before, or in front of you), and the things which shall be hereafter."

Left – Spiritual: Weakness (of man); God's strength or ability demonstrated through man's weakness; rejected (Judges 3:20-21; Judges 20:16; Matthew 25:33).

Left Turn = spiritual change.

North – Spiritual: judgment; Heaven or heavenly;spiritual warfare (as in "taking your inheritance") (Deuteronomy 2:3; Proverbs 25:23; Jeremiah 1:13-14).

Right – Natural: authority, power; the strength of man (flesh) or the power of God revealed through man;accepted, place of favor (Matthew 5:29-30a; Genesis 48:18; Exodus 15:6; Matthew 25:33; 1 Peter 3:22).

Right Turn = natural change.

South – Natural: sin; world; temptation; trial; flesh;corruption; deception (Joshua 10:40; Job 37:9).

West – End (as in the end of the day); grace; death;last (Exodus 10:19). Luke 12:54 "And he said to the people, when you see a cloud (of glory) rise out of the west (grace of God), straightaway ye say, There cometh a shower (blessing); and so it is."

FOOD

Apples – spiritual fruit; temptation; something precious like the apple of God's eyes.

Bread – Jesus Christ (as in the "bread of life"); Word of God; source of nourishment; God's provision.

Grapes – fruitfulness; success in life; evidence of being connected to Christ (as in John 15).

Honey – sweet; strength; wisdom; Spirit of God; the abiding anointing; the sweet Word of our Lord;the best of the land, or abundance.

Lemons – sour; a poor sport.

Manna – God's miraculous provision; something coming directly from God; glory of God; bread of life.

Meat – something meant for the spiritually mature;depth in God's word.

Milk – good nourishment;elementary teaching.

Pears – long life; pear trees have long life;enduring much without complaining.

Pumpkin –Positive: change of the seasons; harvest time;symbol of affection (as in "You are my little pumpkin"); Negative: witchcraft; deception; snare; witch; trick (as in Halloween "trick or treat").

Strawberries – goodness, excellence in nature & virtue; healing; sweet & very humble.

Tomato – kindness, the heart of God; big hearted; generous.

Water – Holy Spirit; refreshing; Word of God; spiritual life.

Wine – Positive: working of the Spirit of God; move of God; Negative: drunkenness; love of the world.

INSECTS

Ant – industrious; wise; diligent; prepared for the future;nuisance; stinging or angry words.

Bee/hornet – painful; strong demonic attack.

Butterfly – freedom; flighty, fragile; temporary glory; transformation.

Flies – evil spirits, filth of Satan's kingdom; Beelzebub -"Lord of the flies"; live on dead things; occult

.

Grasshopper – destruction; drought, or pestilence.

Moth – symbol of destruction; deception (as a moth drawn to the flame)

.Roach – infestation; unclean spirits; hidden sin

.

Scorpion – evil spirits; evil men; pinch of pain.
Spider – occult attack;witchcraft

.

Spider Web – place of demonic attack; ensnaring, confusion. or a trap

KIND OF DOORS

Paper Thin doors: Weakness, tossed and easily blown astray see Eph 4:14 . Tossed to and fro, and carried about with every wind of doctrine.

Steel Doors: closed access; restricted access.

Swing Doors: Allowing anyone access to your life, to your home. Notice that swing doors do not close and they are always open, therefore, it means vulnerability.

MISCELLANEOUS:

Chewing – thinking on something (as in, "I need to chew on that"), meditating; receiving wisdom & understanding.

Choking – hindrance; difficulty in accepting something (as in "the news was hard to swallow"); hatred or anger (as in "I could choke her right now"); unfruitful (as in the weeds growing up and choking the plants).

Christmas – gifts; season of rejoicing; spiritual gifts;surprise; good will; benevolence; commercialism.

Difficulty Chewing – hard saying; difficulty receiving something.

Flying – call or ability of move in the higher things of God; an understanding of navigating the spirit realm.

Kiss – coming into agreement; covenant; seductive process; enticement; deception, betrayal;betrayal from a trusted friend.

childhood home, former high school, – old issues that has never been healed, places from your past;may include former places you have been/lived, and/or former schools, tests, jobs, etc. Reflect on the significance of that season.

Miscarriage – losing something at the preparatory stage, whether good or bad; plans aborted .

Pregnancy – in process of reproducing; preparatory stage; promise of God; Word of God as seed; prophetic word; desire, anticipation, expectancy; purposes of God preparing to come forth

.

Repeating activities – God establishing a matter or issue; repeating because you are not listening

.

Running – faith; perseverance; working out one's salvation; moving forward with purpose.

Swimming – living in the Spirit; moving in the things of the Spirit; operating in the gifts of the Spirit.

MODES OF TRANSPORTATION

Chariot: powerful encounter with the Holy Spirit.

Fast sporty vehicles (mustangs,challengers..etc): represents a fast moving ministry powered by the Spirit.

Ship, steamboat: large ministry; if the ship is not moving, it denotes a lack of the Holy Spirit and the Spirit of God cannot flow through that ministry; complacency, or stagnation.

Steamship Line: (Very Large Boat that carries containers filled with Goods). This symbolizes one who is skilled at trading goods or services, commerce; especially of foreign countries. It also symbolizes someone who is sent to the marketplace.

SUV: large mobile ministry.

OBJECTS

Cell phones, telephones, Television: represents communication with God, communicating with heaven; could also symbolize the flesh.

Check – favor.

Credit Card – presumption; lack of trust; attempting to walk in something that you don't have yet; debt.

Crown – symbol of authority, to reign; seal of power; Jesus Christ; honor, reward.

Dream setting: dark/night time; represents a struggle, trial, trouble, or hidden sin.

Gate – spiritual authority; entrance point for good or evil.

Fruited Trees – healing.

Key – spiritual authority; wisdom; understanding; ability; Jesus.

Ladder – ascending or descending; promotion or demotion; going higher into the things of God; portal of heavenly activity (as in Jacob's ladder had angels ascending and descending).

Microphone – influence; ministry; authority; being heard.

Microwave – impatience; quick work; convenient;sudden.

Mirror – God's Word; a person's heart; vanity.

Money – gain or loss of favor; power; provision;wealth; spiritual riches; authority; strength of man;covetousness; greed.

bank- making spiritual deposits and withdraws

Security Alarms: secure in the spiritual realms, alertness, protection; guarding.

Television – spiritual sight & understanding; entertainment; fleshly cravings & desires; fleshly spirit;love of the world.

Trees – leaders; mature believers; steady.

Roses- This is a symbol of romance, relationship, deep intimacy or bond; negative; seduction, or seducing/enticing.

PEOPLE

Baby – new ministry or responsibility that has recently been birthed; new beginning; new idea; dependent, helpless; innocent; sin.

Bride – Christ's church; covenant, or relationship.

Carpenter – Jesus; someone who makes or mends things; building something spiritually or naturally;preacher.

Giant – Positive: godly men (as in "a giant of the faith"); strong; conquer; Negative: demons; or defilement (as in the Philistine Giant Goliath).

Harlot / Prostitute – a tempting situation; appealing to your flesh; worldly desire; a demon; spirit of lust;spiritual apostasy.

Hijacker – enemy wanting to take control of you or a situation.

Husband – Jesus Christ; actual person.

Lawyer – Positive: Jesus Christ, our advocate; mediator;Negative: Satan, the accuser of the brethren; legalism.

Mob – false accusation.

Policemen – authority for good or evil; protector;spiritual authority.

Prisoner – a lost soul/ condemnation

Shepherd – Jesus Christ; pastor, leader (good or bad); selfless person; protector.

Twins – Positive: double blessing or anointing; Negative: double trouble.

ROOMS IN A HOUSE OR BUILDING

Attic – mind, thought; history; past issues; family history; spiritual realm.

Basement – hidden; forgotten; hidden issues; foundation; basics.

Bathroom – spiritual cleansing; prayer of repentance; confession of sins to another person.

Bathroom in full view – humbling season; others aware of cleansing; transparency.

Bedroom – intimacy; rest; privacy; peace; covenant (as in marriage).

Dining Room/Eating – partaking of spiritual food; fellowship.

Kitchen – heart (as in the "kitchen is the heart of the home"); spiritual preparation; going deep in the Word; spiritual food & feasting.

Restaurant kitchen – teaching ministry; greater influence or impact; preparing to serve people the Word.

Atrium – light & growth from heaven.

Auditorium/Theatre-A place of of performance, prophetic arts, spiritual rhythm and flow within the holy spirit gathering.

Auto Repair Shop – ministry restoration, renewal & repair.

Back porch- The former things of the past or history.

Barn/warehouse – a place of provision & storage.

Bedroom/bed- A place of rest, sleep, paralysis or stagnation, or resting on issues that need to be addressed. Buying, or living in, the house of a known person in the ministry – God has a similar call on your life.

Castle – authority, fortress, or royal residence.

Country General Store – provision; basics, or staples.

Elevator- shifting position in the spirit; going up means to ascend in the spirit or go into higher spiritual realms. Going down in the elevator denotes depression, feeling down, trial/trouble depending on what's happening in the dream could mean demotion.

Front Porch- Vision of the future, or future events that will take place.

Garage – place to rest & refresh; place of protection;or covering for ministries or people.

Garden – a person's heart; love; intimacy; growth.

Gas Station – receiving power; refuelling or "refueling" of the Spirit; empowering.

ramps- struggle

Hallways- spiritual and natural Transition.

Hotel – transition; temporary; place to relax or receive.17

Kitchen- A place or season of preparation.

Library – learning; knowledge; research.

Living room-Learning, gathering of brethren.

Mall – market place; provision for all your needs; Negative – self centeredness; materialism.17

Mobile Home / Trailer House – temporary place, condition or relationship; movement, easily movable;poverty.17

Mountain – place of encountering God; obstacle; difficulty; challenge; Kingdom, or nation.17

Office building – getting things accomplished;productivity.

Park – rest, peace; leisure; God's blessing; vagrancy.

Previous / Old Home – past; inheritance; memory; revisiting old issues.

Prisoners – lost souls; persecuted saints.17

Jail / Prison – bondage; rebellion; addiction.17

Restaurant-A ministry of service/helps; serving spiritual food.

Roof – spiritual covering.17

School- A place or season of learning the spiritual things; being taught about something or someone;teaching ministry, or teaching anointing.

Shack- Poverty mindset; famine; lack; shortage;bankrupt; debt.

Stadium: A ministry of tremendous impact.

Stage-A place of display and god bringing thing to the center of attention; on display; depending on the dreamer, could mean fleshy/soulish/vain.

Staircases- Heavenly portals or dimensions in the spirit. going up; ascending into heaven, greater heights access, authority/rank,promotion. down: demotion, backsliding, failure, rebellion. Play on words: steps that need to be taken.

Swimming pool- a place of spiritual refreshing; god's spirit; immersed in the spirit of god, represents the prophetic, the spirit of prophecy and being immersed in the spirit of prophecy.

Tent – temporary place of rest; meeting place with God.

Theater – on display, visible; going to be shown something; clarity; spiritual sight; fleshly lust.

Two-story House – double anointing.17

Windows – vision; letting light in, spiritual sight, or opportunity (as in an "open window of opportunity").

Zoo – strange; chaos; commotion; very busy place;noisy strife.17.

TRANSPORTATION

Airplane – (size & type of plane correlates to the interpretation) prophetic ministry; going to heights in the Spirit; new & higher understanding.

Armored Car – protection of God.

Automobile – personal ministry or job.

Bicycle – individual ministry or calling requiring perseverance.

Bus – church or ministry/ gathering.

Chariot – major spiritual encounter.

Coal Car – on track; being directed by the Lord.

Convertible – open heaven in your personal ministry or job.

Fire Truck – rescue; putting out fires of destruction.

Fred Flintstone Car – human effort.

Hang glider – going somewhere in the Spirit; driven by the wind of the spirit.

Helicopter – mobile, flexible, or able to get in Spirit quickly.

Limousine: Positive: being taken to your destiny in style;Negative: materialism.

Mickey Mouse Car – purpose is colorful & entertaining.

Minivan – family.

Motorcycle – fast; powerful; maneuverable.

Moving Van – transition; change.

Ocean Liner – impacting large numbers of people.

Riverboat – slow, but impacting many people.
Rollercoaster:

Positive: a wild ride that God is directing, exciting, but temporary;

Negative: a path of destruction that first appears exciting;an emotional trying time with ups and downs.

Sailboats – powered by wind of the Spirit.

Semi-truck – transporting great quantity of goods

Spaceship – to the outer limits, or spiritually speaking.

Speedboat – fast, exciting, or power in the Spirit.

Submarine – undercover and active, but not seen by many; a behind the scenes ministry, or hidden ministry.

Subway – undercover and active, but not seen by many; a behind the scenes ministry, or hidden ministry.

Stagecoach – rough, difficult ride; old way of doing something (good or bad).

Taxi Cab – a shepherd or hireling for someone (driving); paying the price to get where you are going (passenger).

Tow Truck – ministry of helps; gathering the wounded.

Tractor – slow power; may speak about a need to plow.

Train – a movement of God; denomination.

Truck – ability to transport or deliver.

Tugboat – providing assistance; ministry of helps.

WEAPONS

Arrow: Negative: accusation from the enemy. Positive: blessing of children; focus; specific message (as in "shooting an arrow with your life").

Dart – curses; demonic attack; accuracy.

Gun – spiritual authority good or bad; spiritual attack.

Knife – brutal attack or gossip; protection (if you are holding it).

Shield – faith; protection; God's truth; faith in God.

Sword – Word of God; far-reaching; authority.

WEATHER

Dirty Snow – impure.

Earthquake – upheaval; change (by crisis); God's judgment, disaster; trauma, shaking; shock.

Fog – clouded issues or thoughts; uncertainty; confusion; temporary.

Hail – judgment; destruction; bombardment.

Ice/Ice Storm – hard saying; slippery; dangerous.

Rain – blessing; cleansing (clear rain); trouble from enemy (dirty rain).

Snow – blessing; refreshing; righteousness; purity;grace (Isaiah 55:10-11a).

Snow Blizzard – inability to see; storm that blinds you or obstructs your vision.

Snow Drift – barrier; hindrance; opposition.

Storms – disturbance; change; spiritual warfare;judgment; sudden calamity or destruction; turbulent times; trial; opposition.

Tornadoes – destruction, danger; judgment; drastic change; winds of change (negative or positive depending on the color of the tornadoes).

White Storm – God's power; revival, outpouring of the Holy Spirit.

Wind – change (as in "winds of change are blowing");Positive: Holy Spirit. Negative: adversity.

ABOUT THE AUTHOR

Misha Wesley is an Apostolic/Prophetic Voice with accuracy in writing, speaking and releasing on-time prophetic words over cities, regions, and territories. She flows heavy in the gift of healing, deliverance, interpretation of dreams, visions, and numbers.

God has mandated her to teach and bring to Christ unbelievers while also developing, training and equipping each five-fold office. She is the founder of the School of Prophetic Arts and Worship and The Dreamers Publishing House.

The School of Prophetic Arts and Worship is both an online, non-profit Christian based college, located in the Memphis, TN area. This school offers accredited, biblically based, spirit-filled diploma courses, that will awaken the gifts to fullness and birth them forth. Our courses are designed for those who desire to go higher into the prophetic realms of the spirit while delving deeper in intimacy with Jesus Christ.

REFERENCES

1. H2492 - chalam - Strong's Hebrew Lexicon (RSV). Retrieved from https://www.blueletterbible.org// lang/lexicon/lexicon.cfm?Strongs=h2492&t=rsv

2. G3677 - onar - Strong's Greek Lexicon (KJV). Retrieved from https://www.blueletterbible.org// lang/lexicon/lexicon.cfm?Strongs=g3677&t=kjv

3. Derivation. (n.d.). Retrieved March 30, 2018, from https://www.merriam-webster.com/dictionary/ derivation

4. H2451 - chokmah - Strong's Hebrew Lexicon (KJV). Retrieved from https://www. blueletterbible.org//lang/lexicon/lexicon. cfm?Strong's=H02451&t=KJV

5. Wisdom. (1998). In Strong's exhaustive concordance: New American standard Bible. (Updated ed.). Retrieved from http://biblehub.com/hebrew/2452. htm

6. Mastin, L. (2010). Memory Consolidation. Retrieved from http://www.human-memory.net/processes_consolidation.html

7. Oliwenstein, L. (2009, February 25). Caltech Scientists Find Evidence for Precise Communication Across Brain Areas During Sleep. Retrieved from http://www.caltech.edu/news/caltech-scientists-find-evidence-precise-communication-across-brain-areas-during-sleep-1510

8. Bladh, W. (2016, October 16). Sleep Paralysis. Retrieved from https://www.webmd.com/sleep-disorders/guide/sleep-paralysis#1

9. schizophrenia. (2018). Online Etymology Dictionary. Retrieved from https://www.etymonline.com/word/schizophrenia

10. Schizophrenia. (n.d.). Retrieved March 30, 2018, from https://www.merriam-webster.com/dictionary/schizophrenia

11. Moed. (1998). In Strong's exhaustive concordance: New American standard Bible. (Updated.). Retrieved from http://biblehub.com/hebrew/4150.htm

12. Differences between Prophets & seers, (2008, March 21) (By John Paul Jackson a very Sound Prophetic Voice) retrieved from https://seatedprophetic.wordpress.com/prophetic-calling/welcome-2/differences-of-prophets-seers/

12. Spiritual Meanings of the Hebrew Alphabet Letters. (n.d.). Retrieved March 31, 2018, from http://www.walkingkabbalah.com/hebrew-alphabet-letter-meanings/

13. Figure 1. Nun. (n.d.). Retrieved March 31, 2018 from http://www.sofer.co.uk/html/nun_to_samech.html

14. The Ancient Hebrew Alphabet. Adapted from Learn the Ancient Pictographic Hebrew Script by J. Benner (n.d.). Retrieved from http://www.ancient-hebrew.org/learn_ancient.html

15. Voss, U., Holzmann, R., Tuin, I., & Hobson, J. A.(2009). Lucid Dreaming: A State of Consciousness with Features of Both Waking and Non-Lucid Dreaming. Sleep, 32(9), 1191–1200.

16. What Is Lucid Dreaming? A Beginners Overview. (n.d.). Retrieved April 7, 2018, from http://howtolucid.com/lucid-dreaming-definition/

17. Ibojie, J., Jackson, P. J., Goll, J and M., Wolverton, S., Milligan, I. (2018). Biblical Dream Dictionary. Retrieved April 7, 2018, from http://www.unlockingyourdreams.org/dream-dictionary/

18. seven signs of visionary leaders, dreamer achievers academy (2019)https://www.dreamachievers-academy.com/visionary-signs/

19. reference from the holy bible NLT/ https://bible.com/bible/116/isa.45.2-6.NLT

20. orh,chadash-new horizons in jewish experience (2019) zayin-secrets of the hebrew letters-youtube https://www.youtube.com/watch?v=OwA5Jm85E4M

21. hebrew today-news you can use,The Hebrew Alphabet - The Letter Zayin (ז) http://www.hebrewtoday.com/content/hebrew-alphabet-letter-zayin-%D7%96

22. the ancient hebrew alphabet-jeff a benner, (1999-2019) http://www.ancient-hebrew.org/alphabet_letters_lamed.html

INDEX

E

H

I

push, 10
puzzle, 49
python, 109

Q

quickened, 51

R

Raccoon, 112
Rain, 137
Ram, 112
ramps, 130
Rapid Eye Movement, 60
Rat, 112
rattlesnake, 109
Raven, 112
read, 23, 26, 72, 73, 94
Reading Rainbow, 44, 45
REALM, 37, 50
Rebellion, 28, 105
reclassification, 59
Red, 112, 117
reference, 45, 56, 72, 84, 87, 142
reform, 68, 71
refreshed, 79
regions, 5, 37, 49, 71, 139
reign, 17, 69, 74, 125

U

wrath, 85, 102
writing, 73, 139

Y

Yellow, 117
yeshua, 102

Made in the USA
Columbia, SC
05 April 2021